ABOUT THE AUTHOR

Over the last twenty years Karen Kingston has pioneered the western application of Feng Shui and Space Clearing. It is from the workshops and seminars she teaches around the world that her books have emerged.

Karen's most popular seminar, 'Creating Sacred Space', teaches the art of Space Clearing and features a highly motivational segment on clutter clearing. Her workshop, 'Clear Your Clutter with Feng Shui', has been developed from this and is what the material in this book is based on. She also currently teaches a range of Feng Shui and Space Clearing workshops, as well as training Space Clearing and Clutter Clearing consultants.

Born and raised in England, Karen's home since 1990 has been in Bali. She spends six months of each year there, and travels and teaches in the West for the other six months.

KAREN KINGSTON

CLEAR YOUR CLUTTER

WITH

FENG SHUI

~

PIATKUS

© 1998 Karen Kingston

First published in 1998 by
Judy Piatkus (Publishers) Limited
5 Windmill Street
London W1P 1HF

Reprinted in 1998 (three times), 1999

The moral right of the author has been asserted

*A catalogue record for this book is available
from the British Library*

ISBN 0 7499 1824 1

Edited by Carol Franklin
Designed by Sue Ryall

Set by Action Publishing Technology Ltd, Gloucester

Printed and bound in Great Britain by
The Bath Press PLC, Bath, Somerset

CONTENTS

PART TWO IDENTIFYING CLUTTER

PART THREE CLEARING CLUTTER

ACKNOWLEDGEMENTS

I am thankful for the ever-growing network of loving, supportive light-workers I have around me, who have each contributed in some way to help me bring this book into being. My warmest, heartfelt hugs and thanks to you all, and in particular to my dear friends, Gemma Massey, Rowan Hart-Williams, Ni Nyoman Ayu and Richard Norris for your full-on love, companionship and invaluable input to the development of my work. More hugs and thanks to Cathryn McNaughton, Anna Mackenzie, Jean Devlin, Jill Newberry, Katharina Otremba, Kay Tom, Thea Bennett, Nuala Kiernan, Joan McNicholas, the entire team at Piatkus Books, and all the wonderful people I meet along the way who respond with such warmth and enthusiasm to my books and courses, and enrich my journey beyond words.

INTRODUCTION

After my first book, *Creating Sacred Space with Feng Shui*, was published, readers' responses poured in, telling me how much they enjoyed it and what great results they were getting from using the information in it. And there was one chapter in particular which generated more letters, faxes, phone calls and e-mails than any other – the one entitled 'Clearing Clutter'. It seems that everyone has some!

It has therefore been a natural progression to write an entire book on the subject and, being mindful of the nature of the topic, my publishers and I have agreed to make it a reduced size book so as not to increase your clutter quotient too much by purchasing it!

HAPPY CLUTTER CLEARING!

Karen Kingston

PART ONE

UNDERSTANDING
CLUTTER

1

FENG WHAT?

I once met a woman who set off travelling around the planet with little more than the ticket to her first destination in her pocket, but she had one extraordinary skill – the ability to read people's palms – and no matter where she went, she was never short of a place to sleep or food to eat. She would pick a local restaurant or hotel, meet the manager, and offer to do palm readings for guests in return for food, shelter or a small wage. When I met her she had been doing this for three years, had already visited more than a dozen countries, and was having the time of her life.

I have found that Feng Shui has this same universal appeal. When people discover how much their home can affect them, for better or for worse, they are usually fascinated to learn more.

Feng Shui

The rising popularity of Feng Shui in recent years has been extraordinary. I first discovered a passion for working with energy in buildings in the late 1970s and began teaching Feng Shui publicly in 1993. When people asked me then what I did for a living and I told them, their usual response was a puzzled look and a 'Feng WHAT?'. Nowadays they usually nod wisely and the conversation simply glides on. Just about everyone seems to have heard something about it these days.

Feng Shui is the art of balancing and harmonising the flow of natural energies in our surroundings to create beneficial effects in our lives. These natural energy flows were well known and understood by the ancients, and knowledge of them still exists in some cultures today. In Bali, for example, which is my home for half of each year, the people still live in total harmony with both the physical, seen world and the ethereal unseen world of invisible energies. Daily offerings at every household shrine throughout the land and an endless procession of beautiful, powerful and very highly evolved ceremonies in the island's 20,000 communal temples ensures that balance and harmony is maintained. This, to me, is Feng Shui at its best – not just a set of principles applied to an individual building for a specific result, but a whole island of three million people in tune with the sacredness of the land and living Feng Shui as a complete way of life.

My Approach to Feng Shui

My own approach to Feng Shui is rather different to that of other practitioners because I work directly with the energy of each space. Over a twenty-year period, I have developed the ability to see, hear, smell, taste and sense energy in enhanced ways, so to begin a consultation the first thing I usually do is go around the entire inside perimeter of the building, taking an energy reading with my hands. The history of events is recorded in the walls and furniture in the form of subtle electromagnetic imprints, and through reading and interpreting these, I can detect pretty much everything of significance that has ever happened there. Traumatic or repetitive events are embedded the most deeply and have a correspondingly greater effect on present-day occupants. I am also able to find areas where the energy in the building has become stuck and what needs to be done to improve its flow.

Whenever I come across clutter, its energy field is unmistakable. It presents an obstacle to the flow of energy and has an unpleasant, sticky, unclean feel to it, like moving my hands through unseen cobwebs. This is what first made me realise that clutter causes problems in people's lives. It also has a distinctive musty, pervasive odour which I can smell if I walk into someone's home, even if the clutter is hidden away from sight. Actually, if I tune in, I can also smell it in a person's aura (the energy field around their body) if they stand near me, because they become imbued with the smell of it. But don't worry about this if you ever meet me in person

– there is so much clutter in the world that I don't tune in too often!

The good news is that after clearing clutter, this unwholesome, stagnant energy and accompanying odour quickly disappears.

The Feng Shui Bagua

One of the most interesting aspects of Feng Shui, and one which I will be focusing on a great deal in this book, is the Feng Shui 'bagua' grid (see Chapter 8 for a simplified diagram and further information). This can be used to locate where each aspect of your life is found in any building you occupy.

For example, there is an area in your home to do with prosperity. Many people read about Feng Shui or attend a workshop on the subject, get very excited about it, and then rush to put it into practice without realising they need to clear their clutter first. They hear they can hang a mirror in their prosperity corner to attract more wealth. But what if that area is cluttered with junk? Sadly, putting a mirror there is more likely to double their financial problems than resolve them.

This book focuses on just this one aspect of Feng Shui – clearing clutter – which is so vital to its successful application. It is the first book ever to explore this subject in depth in this context, and is intended as an ideal starter for those new to Feng Shui and an invaluable tool for those who have studied it for a while.

Throughout this book I refer mostly to applying the information around your home but of course it can be used equally effectively in your workplace and any other building you occupy.

Space Clearing

Space Clearing is the name I coined[1] many years ago for the branch of Feng Shui that I pioneered and have become best known for. It is the art of clearing and consecrating energies in buildings, and is primarily what my first book was about.

For your life to work well, it is vital to have a good flow of life force energy in your home and workplace. Feng Shui teaches many ways to improve this energy flow and Space Clearing is one of the most effective. It is a simple yet power-ful 21-step ceremony to clear the stuck energies which accumulate in buildings over time and cause you to feel stuck in your own life. The results are impressive, and many people choose to make it part of their regular building maintenance

[1] Interestingly enough, Denise Linn, author of the book *Sacred Space*, independently and 10,000 miles away, also arrived at the same name for similar energy-clearing ceremonies she pioneered and developed! Since the publication of her book and my book *Creating Sacred Space with Feng Shui*, other people have also started using the name Space Clearing to describe all manner of weird and wonderful ceremonies. In this book, all references to Space Clearing refer specifically to the ceremony I describe in my own book, of which I can guarantee the effectiveness.

programme so that the space is energetically as well as physically clean and clear. There are very few buildings which are so well designed that they don't benefit from having this done regularly, and Feng Shui always works better and faster when done in conjunction with Space Clearing.

There are three main causes of stuck energy which Space Clearing addresses:

★ physical grime
★ predecessor energy
★ clutter

Physical grime   By this I mean all types of dirt, dust, filth, grot, grease, gunge, crud and general yuck. Low level energy always accumulates around dirt, hence the old adage 'cleanliness is next to godliness'. Having a good clean-up is an essential part of Space Clearing.

Predecessor energy   Everything that happens in a building is recorded in the walls, floors, furniture and objects in the space. This builds up in layers, in much the same way as grime does, except that we cannot see it, and it affects us in profound ways. For example, if you move into a home where the previous occupants were happily married, it is likely that you, too, will find marital bliss there. If, on the other hand, you or the previous occupants have been unhappy, divorced, ill, gone bankrupt, put on weight, or any of a million other things, those energies remain in the building and will generally cause history to repeat itself. These lingering frequencies create stuckness of the kind you would certainly want to clear.

Clutter Any kind of clutter creates an obstacle to the smooth flow of energy around a space. This in turn creates stuckness and/or confusion in the lives of the occupants.

While the Space Clearing ceremony to clear predecessor energy can easily be accomplished in a few hours, the cleaning and clutter clearing aspects can take some people a while longer. In fact, it is fairly common for me to hear from readers that they glided through the early chapters of my first book, came to the clutter chapter, and there the bookmark stayed for six months or more until they had done enough work to read on!

These are the kinds of letters I get:

'I have now cleared out most of the clutter and am ready to do the Space Clearing ceremony. I feel that in the last six months I have not only sorted through every cupboard in my home but also through every part of my life. I already feel healthier and happier than I have felt in years.'

'I read the clutter chapter in your book and am now on my fourteenth rubbish bag and still going strong. My husband is astounded because he has been nagging me for years to do this.'

'I thought one skip would do it but I am now on my third. How did I ever let things get to this state?'

'Your book inspired me to clear out my junk room and have a car boot sale. I made £300. That inspired me to clear out my garage, and I made over £600. I have used the money to take my first holiday in years and I'm sending you this postcard to say "thank you"!'

The next chapter will start to explain more fully why most of your lovely clutter is more of a hindrance in your life than a help.

2

THE PROBLEM WITH CLUTTER

In the course of doing Feng Shui, Space Clearing and Clutter Clearing consultations, I have the opportunity to visit many homes and poke about in places people would never let me otherwise. As a result of this unusual (and sometimes dubious!) privilege I have been able, over the years, to identify and verify the type of problems clutter causes.

Clutter and Feng Shui

It is important to realise how fundamentally intrinsic clutter clearing is to the whole practice of Feng Shui. Most books on the subject mention it only in passing or not at all. Perhaps they assume their readers have already dealt with this issue, but of course the truth is that most have not.

I do not consider clutter clearing to be one process and Feng Shui to be another. I have come to realise that clutter clearing is one of the most powerful, transformative aspects of Feng Shui there is, and in most cases, Feng Shui cures and enhancements are at best only minimally effective until this has been done.

If you have already been using Feng Shui for years without knowing this you will be delighted at the energy upsurge clearing your clutter will bring about. And if you are new to Feng Shui, you will be pleasantly surprised to realise that the first and most important steps to learning these arts are already well within your reach.

Clutter is Stuck Energy

The word 'clutter' derives from the Middle English word 'clotter', which means to coagulate – and that's about as stuck as you can get.

Clutter accumulates when energy stagnates and, likewise, energy stagnates when clutter accumulates. So the clutter begins as a symptom of what is happening with you in your life and then becomes part of the problem itself because the more of it you have, the more stagnant energy it attracts to itself.

You know what it is like. You are walking down the street and you see that someone has thoughtlessly thrown an empty cigarette packet in a corner near the roadside. The next day you walk past the same spot, and the empty pack has been joined by a few more items of rubbish. Before long it becomes a full-blown garbage dump. Clutter accumulates in the same way in your home. It starts with a bit and then it slowly, insidiously, grows and grows – and so does the stagnant energy around it, which then has a corresponding stagnating effect on your life.

If you somehow get your life moving again, you will instinctively want to clear the clutter out of your home and make a fresh start. It will feel like the obvious thing to do. So one approach to clearing clutter is to embark on a course of self-improvement and wait until you get to the stage where you just can't stand having clutter around you any more. There are many self-improvement books you can read and courses you can take (and I certainly recommend that you do), but it can take a while for you to get inspired enough to clear your clutter taking this route.

What I am teaching in this book is a new approach – sorting out your life by sorting out your junk, which results in a tremendous renewal of your life force energy. This is something practical and tangible you can do actively to help yourself.

Stuck Energy is Very Sticky

This is why it is easy to let your clutter stay put. You have to have some pretty good reasons to rouse yourself enough to do anything about it. That's what the next chapter's about.

3

THE EFFECTIVENESS OF CLUTTER CLEARING

Every aspect of your life is anchored energetically in your living space, so clearing your clutter can completely transform your entire existence.

Clean Up Your Life

Back in the 1980s, I was one of the top professional rebirthers in London (rebirthing is a way of releasing inner blockages through the breath). I have always been a great one for motivating people to help themselves, and I began to suggest de-cluttering as extra 'homework' for some of my clients who were particularly stuck in their lives. Sure enough, in the process of sorting out their own belongings, they made substantial inroads into sorting out themselves. For the really stubborn cases I would tell them at the end of a session that next week I would be rebirthing them at their home, not mine. I think it was realising the difference between how their home felt and how mine felt that shamed them into action.

One particular long-term client I remember was a young girl who was a recovering heroin addict. After she had had a couple of relapses I realised I had to take a firmer approach. I refused to work with her again unless we did a session at her home and she showed her commitment to kicking her habit by getting her place fit to do a rebirthing session in. This was very tough for her to do. Her self-esteem had sunk so low over the years that she was living in squalor. But she set to work with a will and triumphantly invited me to her flat several weeks later. It was plain to see how much work had been done, and the change in her in those weeks was also remarkable. The next few therapy sessions marked profound breakthroughs for her.

Several years later I bumped into her in a public place and didn't recognise her. She had transformed into a radiantly beautiful woman, full of happiness and love for life, with a successful career doing what she had always dreamed of doing. She dated the change from those sessions and told me she had never touched heroin or looked back since. Through clearing out her clutter she had cleaned up her life.

You and Your Home

The reason why clutter clearing is so effective is that while you are putting your external world in order there are corresponding changes going on internally too. Everything around you, especially your home environment, mirrors your inner self. So by changing your home you also change the possibilities in your own life. Removing the obstacles to the harmonious flow of energy in your living environment creates more harmony in your life and the space for wonderful new opportunities to come to you.

Go For It!

One woman who came to one of my workshops got so inspired that she went home and phoned up Oxfam and said, 'You are going to need to send a lorry!'. She cleared out all but five items of clothing from her wardrobe, her ancient stereo system, and stacks and stacks of junk. In doing this, she released huge amounts of stuck energy, which created space for something new to come in. A week later she received a cheque in the post from her mother for £5,000, and she went straight out and bought herself a whole new wardrobe of wonderful clothes, a new sound system and everything else she wanted.

She told me the cheque was totally unexpected, and that the last time her mother had sent her any money was ten years earlier! I don't recommend that everyone does this, but it certainly worked for her.

Here's an inspiring letter I received from a woman called

Susan Byron, who lives in Ireland. She read my book and also went for clutter clearing in a big way:

> 'I heard you on the radio this morning and I just had to write and tell you that I am moving house tomorrow and the only possessions I will be taking apart from the husband, kids, favourite plants and animals is your book, my candles, incense and bell.
>
> 'So many wonderful things have happened to me since your book fell into my hands three months ago and I space cleared my house. I kept a diary and it listed over a hundred in about two weeks. To cut a long story short, we have since accomplished our ambition to move to County Clare on the West coast, finished our house, sold it and put a deposit on a beautiful site on the Atlantic, lots of obstacles have been overcome quite effortlessly and recurring problems stopped.'

Another person wrote to tell me:

> 'I have read your book … and have now cleared out most of the clutter and would like to undertake the full Space Clearing procedure. Since I first began clearing out two weeks ago, I have had three small wins, two on the lottery and one in a raffle – as I rarely if ever win anything, this could hardly be coincidence!'

These kinds of letters arrive in my mailbox every day and are what has inspired me to actually write this book.

4

WHAT IS CLUTTER
EXACTLY?

The Oxford dictionary defines clutter as 'a crowded and untidy collection of things'. Yes, that's a part of it but it only describes clutter at the purely physical level.

In my definition there are four categories of clutter:

★ Things you do not use or love
★ Things which are untidy or disorganised
★ Too many things in too small a space
★ Anything unfinished.

Let's have a look at each of these so that you will be in no doubt as you read through this book where your own focus for clutter clearing needs to be.

Things You do not Use or Love

Things which are loved, used and appreciated have strong, vibrant, joyous energies around them, which allow the energy in the space to flow through and around them. If you have a clear focus in your life and you surround yourself with things which have this marvellous free-flowing energy, you will have a correspondingly happy, joyous, free-flowing life. Conversely, anything neglected, forgotten, unwanted, unloved or unused will cause the energy in your home to slow and stagnate, and then you will feel that your life is not moving.

You are connected to everything you own by fine strands of energy. When your home is filled with things which you love or use well it becomes an incredible source of support and nourishment for you. Clutter, on the other hand, drags your energy down and the longer you keep it, the more it will affect you. When you get rid of everything which has no real meaning or significance for you, you literally feel lighter in body, mind and spirit.

Things Which are Untidy or Disorganised

This category is for the messy people of the world and the hopelessly disorganised. Even if you keep your stuff honed down to just the things you use and love, your place will still be cluttered if they are scattered all over the place and it's difficult to find items when you want them. Probably, like most messies, you maintain there is order in your chaos and, what's more, you need to keep things in the open to remind you of important things you have to do. But if someone actually puts you to the test and asks you where something is, at best you only know the general direction and rarely the precise location.

Everyone's life works better when they know where things are. For example, think of your bed. The energy connection between you and it is direct and clear. Unless you are the nomadic type, you know exactly where it is and you can connect to it mentally in micro-seconds. Now think about your house keys. Do you know exactly where they are or do you have to mentally hunt around for them? How about that letter you need to reply to? Where is it? When your things get jumbled up and confused, the strands between you and them become like entangled spaghetti. This creates stress and confusion in your life rather than the peace and clarity which comes from knowing where things are.

Clutter in this category consists of things which either don't have a proper place of their own or do have one but have strayed from it and got all mixed up with everything else. Many of the items seem to just appear in your life rather than you making a conscious decision to acquire them. They include the mail which relentlessly pops through your letter-box and dauntingly distributes itself in far-flung corners of your home, and other bits of paper which appear from nowhere and build themselves into mountainous heaps, defiantly resisting all your attempts to categorise and sort them. Then there are those impulse buys. You bring them home and say to yourself, 'I'll just put it there for now' and there it stays. Sometimes it can stay there for months, years or even decades, always looking slightly out of place and vaguely irking you at the back of your mind.

Now, I'm not advocating pristine neatness. A home which is too tidy, where everything is 'just so', is energetically sterile and can be as much of a problem as a place that is a complete tip. But your home is an outward representation of what is going on inside you, so if you are messy on the outside there is a corresponding mess of some kind on the inside too. By sorting out the outer, the inner starts slotting neatly into place.

Too Many Things in Too Small a Space

Sometimes the problem is simply one of space. Your life or your family has expanded but your home has stayed the same size, or it never was big enough in the first place. You can become creative with storage units but the more you cram in to your living space, the less room there is for energy to move and the more difficult it becomes to get anything done. With clutter of the just-too-much-for-the-amount-of-space variety, your home starts to feel as if it cannot breathe, your own breathing will actually become tighter and shallower (when was the last time you took a really deep breath and filled your lungs?), and you will feel constricted in what you can do in your life.

The only solution is to move to a bigger place or shift some of your stuff off the premises. You will be amazed at how good it feels, either way.

Anything Unfinished

This form of clutter is harder to see and easier to ignore than the other types, but its effects are far-reaching. Anything unfinished in the physical, mental, emotional and spiritual realms clutters your psyche.

Things not dealt with in your home reflect issues not dealt with in your life, and they are a constant drain on your energy. There are the niggly repairs such as fixing the broken drawer, mending the broken appliance, repairing the tap that keeps dripping, and the bigger jobs, such as redecorating the house, servicing the central heating or taming the jungle that has become your garden. The larger the scale, the more these things impinge on your ability to get on with your life.

Buttons which need sewing on, phone calls you need to make, relationships you need to move on from, and many other different forms of loose ends in your life will hinder your progress if you do not deal with them. Your subconscious mind will suppress these things nicely for you if you ask it to but it takes a lot of your energy to do so. You will be amazed at how your vitality levels soar if you complete all your unfinished business.

The next chapter explores how all these types of clutter actually affect you in your life in ways you may never have suspected.

5

How Clutter Affects You

Most people have no idea how much their clutter affects them. You may actually fondly believe yours to be an asset, or at least a potential asset after it has been sorted through and organised. It is only when you start clearing it out that you will realise how much better you feel without it.

Clutter will affect you according to the type of person you are, how much of the stuff you have, where in your home you keep it and how long you have had it. Here are some of the main effects to watch out for:

Having Clutter Makes You Feel Tired and Lethargic

Most people who hoard clutter say they can't find the energy to begin to clear it. They constantly feel tired. But the stagnant energy which stacks up around clutter actually causes tiredness and lethargy. Clearing it frees up the energy in your home and releases new vitality in your body. Here is what people tell me:

'I stayed up late to read your book and go so "wired" that I couldn't sleep. Finally I got out of bed and started clearing my clutter until 4 in the morning! I had to go to work the next day but I didn't feel at all tired.'

'I used to be a couch potato. I would come home from work and just "veg out" in front of the TV every night. I did a major clutter clearing purge and now I find I have so little use for my television that I have thrown it out. I have so many new interests I don't have time to watch it.'

'At first I felt daunted by the sheer volume of my clutter but I knew I had to clear it. What amazes me is how much better I feel after each drawer, and how the energy somehow comes from nowhere to carry on and do more.'

Having Clutter Keeps You in the Past

When all your available space is filled with clutter, there is no room for anything new to come into your life. Your thoughts tend to dwell in the past, and you feel bogged down with problems which have dogged you for some time. You tend to look back rather than forward in your life, blaming the past for your current situation rather than taking responsibility for creating a better tomorrow. Clearing your clutter allows you to begin to deal with your problems and move forward. You have to release the past to create a better tomorrow.

Having Clutter Congests Your Body

When you have lots of clutter, the energy of your home gets congested and so does your body. Clutterbugs generally do not take enough exercise, are often constipated, have dull, clogged complexions and no vitality in their eyes. People with little clutter in their lives are generally more active, have clear, radiant skin and a twinkle in their eyes. The choice is yours.

Having Clutter Can Affect Your Body Weight

A curious fact I have noticed over the years is that people who have lots of clutter in their homes are usually over-weight. I believe this is because both body fat and clutter are forms of self-protection. By building layers of fat or clutter around yourself, you hope to cushion yourself against the shocks of life, and particularly against emotions you have difficulty handling. It gives you the illusion of being able to control things and prevent them from affecting you too deeply. But it is an illusion. In Oprah Winfrey's words:

> 'What I've learned through my thirteen-year ordeal with weight is that you can't really begin to work on the physical until you first get at what's holding you back emotionally. The reason we don't move forward in our lives is because of the fears that hold us back, the things that keep us from being all that we were meant to be.'

I have certainly found it to be true that overweight people often have many fears they have buried deep inside themselves which they need to overcome to clear their clutter. However, many write to let me know how liberating it feels when they finally do it, and how the process of letting go of their junk also magically allows them to let go of their fat. They tell me it is also a darn sight easier to focus on dieting their home than dieting their body and when they start looking after their environment more they naturally feel more inclined to look after themselves better too. As one woman put it, 'After you have cleared the junk out of your home, it doesn't feel right to keep putting junk food in your body.'

Having Clutter Confuses You

When you live surrounded by clutter, it is impossible to have clarity about what you are doing in your life. When you clear it, you get fewer colds, you can think more clearly and life decisions become easier. Being clear of clutter is one of the greatest aids I know to discovering and manifesting the life you want.

Having Clutter Affects the Way People Treat You

People treat you the way you treat yourself. So if you value yourself and look after yourself, people will treat you well. If you 'let yourself go' and allow the junk to mount up around you, you may attract people who mistreat you in some way because subconsciously you will feel that is what you deserve.

If your home is untidy as well as cluttered, your friends may like you as a person but it may be difficult for them to really respect you, especially if you are always behind with everything you need to do, don't keep your promises because you are disorganised, and so on. When you sort out your home you can improve all your relationships in the process.

Having Clutter Makes You Procrastinate

If you have a lot of clutter, you will tend to put off doing things until tomorrow. The clutter stagnates your energy and makes it difficult to get yourself to do anything. After clutter clearing you are likely to surprise yourself (and everyone else!) by wanting to do things you have put off for a long time. People suddenly feel motivated to replant the garden, take up a study course, take a holiday, and so on. The letters I receive on just this one effect of clearing clutter are amazing!

'My husband died five years ago and I kept delaying clearing out his belongings. Your book finally gave me the courage to pack up all his clothes and take them to Oxfam, and it was as if a fresh breath of air came into my life. I know it's hard to believe at my age (I'm 71) but I have enrolled at college to learn about computers and may soon be the world's first cybergranny!'

'Whilst sorting through my attic, I came across letters from some dear old friends who had moved abroad, and found tears rolling down my cheeks as I realised how much I missed them and regretted losing touch with them. To cut a long story short, I polished off the attic and caught a plane to go and see them. We had the most wonderful reunion. I am now seriously thinking of moving out there myself.'

'This clutter clearing thing seems to get into your blood. Not content with clearing out every cupboard in my entire house, I am now up at dawn every morning tidying up the garden. Where will this end?'

Having Clutter Causes Disharmony

Clutter is a major cause of arguments in families, flat-shares, and between partners and co-workers. If you live or work knee-deep in the stuff and those around you do not, their lifestyle will not impede your progress but yours most certainly can impede theirs.

If you know anything about metaphysics you will understand that all these people attracted you into their life for a reason, and you attracted them into your life for a reason. But the clutter is a low level reason. Clear it out and then you will be able to get to the higher purpose of why you are together, which is much more interesting than arguing about mundane junk!

Having Clutter Can Make You Feel Ashamed

Perhaps you have reached the stage where your home is so cluttered and such a mess that you are ashamed to invite people round, and positively panic if anyone turns up unannounced. You can live in lonely isolation with your junk, but wouldn't you prefer to have a good clear out, repair your self-esteem and regenerate your social life with confidence?

Having Clutter Can Put Your Life on Hold

One lovely elderly couple I met were living in a beautiful fifteen-room mansion. Their children had all grown up and left home, and they enjoyed a happy, loving marriage. The living areas and bedrooms belonging to each of their children were tidy and well maintained, but over a period of time, most of their own bedroom and three of their other rooms had completely vanished under a sea of clutter. One room looked like a junk shop, with ornaments and knick-knacks of every description stacked up in piles, another room was heaped waist-high with mounds of clothes, and the third room had more of their own junk and boxes of things inherited from an aunt which 'needed sorting'. When questioned they admitted that they would love to travel and enjoy the last years of their lives together, but nagging away at the back of their minds all the time were these unsorted junk rooms. Whenever the question of taking a holiday came up, they decided they couldn't do it until the junk had been sorted first. In effect, their shame about their clutter had kept them at home for years!

Don't let your life slip away. Sit down right now and write a list of all the things you would love to do if only your clutter were sorted, and let this be the inspiration for you to get on with it.

Having Clutter Depresses You

The stagnant energy of clutter pulls your energy down and can make you feel depressed. In fact I have yet to meet a depressed person who doesn't surround themselves with clutter. Feelings of hopelessness are compounded by clutter and can be relieved to some extent by clearing it because you create space for something new to come into your life (most types of depression are caused by your Higher Self stopping you doing what you have been doing because it is time for you to do something else).

If you are so depressed that you can't even begin to think about having a clear-out, at least get your clutter off the ground (depressed people tend to stack their clutter at a low level), which will lift your energy and your spirits too. It would also be a good idea to have your home checked for geopathic stress (harmful energy which radiates up from the earth). Clutter often accumulates in geopathically stressed areas, and it may well be a causative factor in your depression too. See the chapter about Geopathic Stress in my first book, *Creating Sacred Space with Feng Shui*.

Having Clutter Creates Excess Baggage

If you have a lot of clutter at home then you will certainly want to take a lot of it with you when you travel. Clutterholics often have to pay excess baggage charges for all the things they drag on holiday with them 'just in case' they need them, not to mention all the souvenirs they buy to bring back home.

They tend to create excess baggage of the emotional kind too. Do you make mountains out of molehills, create dramas unnecessarily, get upset at imagined slights? Learn to lighten up physically and discover you can lighten up emotionally too, and enjoy your life much more.

Having Clutter Dulls Your Sensitivity and Enjoyment of Life

Just as clutter mutes the sounds and the atmosphere in your home, it also mutes your ability to live life to the full. You can become a creature of habit and feel like you are living in a rut, just doing the same thing, day after day, year after year. You may even become a boring person to know. Clearing the clutter allows the fresh winds of inspiration to enter your home and your life. Even moving it around your home from time to time will help to refresh the energy.

A major clear-out is absolutely essential if you truly want to have passion, joy and happiness in your life. These feelings are the experience of great energy flowing through your body and this cannot happen if your channels are clogged.

Having Clutter Causes Extra Cleaning

It takes at least twice as long to clean a place that is cluttered with objects and, not only that, the objects themselves also need cleaning. The more clutter you have, the more dust accumulates, the more the energy stagnates and the less inclined you are to do your cleaning. It's a downward spiral. Just think of all the fun things you could do in your life if you let go of your clutter and cut your cleaning time in half!

Having Clutter Makes You Disorganised

How often do you lose your keys, glasses, wallet? How many time have you searched for something, finally given up and eventually come across it weeks or months later? Or maybe it is usually easier for you to go out and buy a replacement rather than keep looking for the one you know you have?

Being disorganised wastes time, which is frustrating and makes you feel like a failure. Many people stay disorganised as a long-standing protest against parental discipline enforced when they were young, but to continue this all your life only sabotages you. It is very empowering to decide to take control of your home and do what you want to do, instead of allowing unresolved issues from your childhood to run your life.

Having Clutter Can Be a Health or Fire Hazard

It can come to this. When clutter starts to smell bad, attracts vermin, becomes damp, mildewed or starts to disintegrate in some other way, it becomes unhygienic to keep it – for you and also for your neighbours. Some types of clutter can also be a fire risk.

If you value your own health and safety, and would prefer to stay on good terms with your neighbours, clear it all out before it gets any worse (it certainly won't get better by itself!).

Having Clutter Can Create Undesirable Symbology

What message does your clutter send out symbolically? Feng Shui teaches us to be very selective about the ornaments, pictures and photographs we have around us, which all give out a message. It is amazing to me how often people cling to objects which they say have great sentimental value and yet symbolically represent exactly what they say they no longer want.

To take a simple example, if you are single and looking for a new partner, dump your single ornaments and solitary portraits, and replace them with paired objects and pictures of couples. If you are prone to arguments, don't have much red in your decor. If you feel depressed, get rid of all the downward-hanging things in your home and replace them with upward-surging objects which lift your energy. Read the chapter later in this book entitled 'Clutter and Feng Shui Symbology', and you may want to wipe out half your clutter in one go when you discover it is sending out the wrong frequencies for what you want in your life!

Having Clutter Costs You Financially

What does it actually cost you to keep the stuff? Sometimes, when all other reasoning has failed, it is the simple financial mathematics which bring people to their senses about their clutter.

Let's do some sums. Go into each room of your home and estimate the percentage of space that is taken up by things you rarely or never use. Be very honest with yourself as you do this process. If you want the blatant truth, include everything you don't absolutely love or haven't used in the last year; for a more gentle approach, extend the time period to two or three years. In an average-sized home, you may end up with a list that looks something like this:

1	Entrance foyer	5%
2	Sitting room	10%
3	Dining room	10%
4	Kitchen	30%
5	Bedroom 1	40%
6	Bedroom 2	25%
7	Junk room	100%
8	Bathroom	15%
9	Cellar	90%
10	Attic	100%
11	Garden shed	60%
12	Garage	80%
	Total clutter	565%

Now divide the total by the number of areas.

565 per cent ÷ 12 areas = average 47 per cent junk per room!

So, in this example, the cost of storing clutter works out to a staggering 47 per cent of the cost of the rent or mortgage for your home. I seriously suggest you do your own sums right now.

Perhaps you have even reached the stage where your stuff has overflowed your home and you are also paying premium rentals for commercial storage space elsewhere. Owners of these depots report booming business in recent years. In urban areas it is often necessary to book several months ahead if you want to rent secure storage space. Is this really a worthwhile use of your money? Isn't there something else you would much rather spend it on?

And there are other ways in which your clutter habit costs you. There is the cost of your time shopping for it and finding a place to put it when you get home. There is often the expense of buying something to store it in. We are talking here about things like storage boxes, shelving, cupboards, wardrobes, drawers, filing cabinets, trunks or, in more extreme cases, building a back extension, erecting a garden shed, installing flooring in the attic or constructing a second garage. Then there is the cost of cleaning it, maintaining it at the right temperature and humidity, protecting it from weather and pest damage and transporting it when you move house. You may also decide to insure it and install a security system to guard it. Finally there is the time, expense and emotional energy it costs to get rid of it when you eventually come to your senses. Is it really worth it?

All these costs frequently total more than the actual items themselves. Think about it. You are expending all that time, money and effort to buy things you will never use and then paying to keep them indefinitely for no reason!

Having Clutter Distracts You from Important Things

Do you own your stuff or does it own you? Everything you own has a call on your attention, and the more clutter you have, the more your energy is tied up in mundane matters. As the last section showed, it all needs taking care of in some way. When you clear out your clutter, you leave yourself free to put the important things of your life in perspective rather than being constantly bogged down in the details of day-to-day maintenance.

Understanding how your clutter can affect you helps you to look at it in a new way and start to make new decisions about whether you want to keep it or not. A vital part of that decision-making process also involves understanding why you accumulated the clutter in the first place, which is what the next chapter is about.

6

SO WHY DO PEOPLE KEEP CLUTTER?

The answer to this question is complex, and as you read through the following pages you will find that the different sections resonate with you to a greater or lesser degree.

In all the many consultations I have done to help people clear their clutter, the junk itself is only the physical aspect of the problem. There are always many layers of deeper issues underlying the reason why clutter has accumulated. Excuses such as 'I'm too busy/lazy/stressed' are all red herrings. If you make time to acquire clutter (and people easily do that) then you can also make the time to clear it. These defences are attempts to evade the issue without having to look at the psychological reasons for hoarding.

Before going any further with this, let me say first that I

firmly believe that everyone is always doing the best they know how. So let's take judgement about clutter – your own and everyone else's – and dump it right now. You can also unload any guilt you may feel. If you have clutter in your life then for some reason you have needed to create it. Therefore, the clutter you now have has been perfect for you in your life until this point.

The purpose of this chapter is to help you understand why you have needed clutter in the past, which will help you to release it and cease to accumulate it in the future. These patterns are buried deep in your subconscious mind and, without you realising it, they are running your life. After you become aware of them, they gradually lose their power over you, and soon you will even be able to look back and laugh at your previous clutter-hoarding antics.

So let's have a look at some of the reasons why you may have felt the need to keep the stuff you have.

Keeping Things 'Just in Case'

This is the Number One reason that people give for keeping clutter. 'I can't throw it away,' they plead, 'because it is sure to come in useful some day.' By all means keep reasonable stocks of the things you use regularly, but do you really need all those (fill in the blank yourself) you have been keeping all these years?

'Who knows?' you reply, remembering all the times you threw something out and then found you needed it after all.

So let me explain to you now why this happens and how to change it.

Keeping things 'just in case' indicates a lack of trust in the future. You create your own reality by the thoughts you have, so if you worry that you will need something after you have thrown it away then sure enough, very soon afterwards, your subconscious mind will create a situation where you need that very thing, however obscure it may be. 'I *knew* it would come in useful some time!' you exclaim, but in actual fact you could have averted this need by thinking differently. You created that need yourself by believing that you would have it! If you have lots of clutter you are hanging on to because you think like this, you are sending out a message to the universe that you don't trust it to provide for you, and you will always feel vulnerable and insecure about the future.

Often it is not just your own future you are concerned about providing for. You may also sincerely want to be able to help others in need. So then you save absolutely everything 'just in case' someone else needs it. Now you are saving things on behalf of people you may not even know yet and situations which will probably never happen. This makes it virtually impossible to throw anything away!

Here are some of the most poignant examples of the 'this-may-come-in-useful-some-day' type of clutter I have come across so far:

★ Five aquariums being kept in an attic for fifteen years by a man who didn't like fish!

★ A whole pantry stacked full to the ceiling with empty bottles, margarine cartons, egg boxes and the like, none of which had *ever* come in useful in over twenty years.

★ A large playroom full of children's toys being kept for the future offspring of the couple's gay son, 'just in case' he ever changed his mind and decided to marry a woman and have babies.

★ A complete set of UK telephone directories (several dozen volumes) for the year 1981 (spotted in 1997!).

If you dig around in your home, you will probably find your own absurd items to add to this list.

The wonderful thing is that once you fully understand your own role in creating the sudden need for things you have finally decided to get rid of, it stops happening that way. Then, when you decide to let things go, you either never need them again or, if you do need them, similar or better things will somehow turn up in your life at the right time. There's a certain knack to this, it's true, but anyone can learn it. The more you can learn to trust that life will take care of you, the more life will take care of you.

Identity

Another reason you can get attached to your belongings is because you somehow feel that your own identity is tied up in them. You can look at a ticket stub from a performance you went to ten years ago and say, 'Yes, I was there, I did that'.

You can look at an ornament given to you by a friend and say, 'Yes, I had a friend who cared enough about me to give me this'. By keeping these reminders around you, you may feel more secure in who you are.

It is fine to keep some gifts and mementoes of happy times, providing they still have current value for you and there are not so many of them that they anchor your energy too much in the past instead of the present. You can ensure this by having regular clear-outs to keep the things you surround yourself with up to date with who you have become.

However, clearing out these types of belongings presents unique difficulties. You sometimes identify with them so strongly that you feel you are throwing a part of yourself away or, if it was a gift from a friend, that you are throwing your friend's kindness away. This accounts for the many ambivalent feelings about clearing sentimental clutter and, to a certain extent, these feelings are valid. Our possessions do become filled with our own frequencies and the things we use often, feel fond of or created ourselves are particularly permeated with our own energy. Gifts from friends (especially treasured items that they 'want you to have') are permeated with their energy. This, incidentally, is one of the deeper reasons why people feel so emotionally devastated when they lose everything as a result of theft, fire, flood or other so-called disaster. They are grieving for the parts of themselves and the friends they have lost with the possessions (although actually these are wonderful heaven-sent opportunities, co-created with their Higher Self, to give them a fresh start in life).

The fact is that our own continuance and well-being does not depend on any objects continuing to be in our possession. It is perfectly OK to let these things go. If you identify very strongly with certain things and you want to make it easier on yourself, see that they go to a good new home. Let them go with love, and give them to someone who will appreciate and use them. In this way, you will eventually come to feel guiltier about holding on to them than letting them go, because if you hold on you become the obstacle to them having a whole new lease of life with someone who will really value them!

Status

This is otherwise known as 'keeping up with the Joneses' and serves the function of bolstering low self-esteem. Now I am not saying that everyone who lives in a grand mansion has low self-esteem. Far from it. But some people do create the trappings of prosperity around them simply to 'keep up appearances' and no amount of 'stuff' will ever be enough until they tackle the deeper issues of self-worth.

It is so easy in the possession-orientated western culture to lose track of who you are and why you are here. Nowhere is this more evident than in the USA, where personal status is so often defined, not by who you are, but by what you are worth. However, if you own things for this reason, you are buying into an illusion, for you cannot take any of it with you when you go. Your status as an eternal spirit is defined by an entirely different set of principles than those set by our transient materialistic world.

Security

While it is reasonable to have a basic nesting instinct and create a home which serves your needs, there is a point where the motivation for acquiring things goes off track. Modern advertising is deliberately designed to play on our insecurities. 'If you don't have one of these you will be a lesser human being' is one of the consistent underlying messages we receive. To discover just how much you are influenced, I challenge you to try not to read the advertising billboards next time you go down the street. Unless you are in a country where you don't understand the language, this is very difficult to do. These multi-million dollar advertising messages relentlessly condition us in very persuasive ways without us ever realising it. We are bombarded by them – television, radio, newspapers, magazines, posters, car bumpers, tee-shirts, the internet, you name it – all encouraging us to buy, buy, buy.

But here's the thing – no matter how many possessions you have, you never feel secure. As soon as you get one thing, there is always something else you 'need'. And also, you have the added problem of worrying about losing the stuff you already have. Some of the most insecure people I know are multi-millionaires. True security can only come from knowing who you are and what you are here to do.

Territorialism

Let's look at what happens when you decide to buy something new. Suppose you are out shopping, looking for a new jacket. You find one you really like, leave it for a moment to check that there isn't one you like better, and along comes another shopper who picks up the jacket and looks interested in buying it. Panic wells up inside you – 'That's MY jacket' you are thinking. And then there is the relief when they put it down and move on, or the awkwardness of butting in and telling them you were there first. These feelings can be very intense, but realistically it's only a jacket which minutes before meant nothing to you.

Then you buy it, take it home, and the energy connection strengthens. If the next day it gets accidentally stained, ripped, mangled by a passing elephant, or whatever, it can be calamity! disaster! heartbreak! And yet, two days previously, before it came into your life, it meant nothing to you. What's going on?

This territorialism and desire to possess things comes directly from the ego, which strives to own and control things. Your spirit already knows you own nothing. It is a matter of realising that your happiness does not depend on your ownership of things. They can help you in your journey but they are not the journey itself.

Inherited Clutteritis

We learn most of our behaviour patterns from our parents. And if one or both of your parents were clutterholics, the chances are that their parents before them were too, and their parents before them were too. These patterns are passed down through the generations.

So that you can appreciate the immensity of what you are up against if you come from a long line of clutterholics, let me relate an astonishing fact I came across recently. If you go back just six hundred years in your family tree, which is about twenty generations, and if each of your clutterbug forerunners replaced themselves by producing two offspring with their spouse, then the total number of your direct ancestors since the year 1400 AD totals over one million people. That's a lot of clutterholism to contend with.

The 'just in case' mentality is part of the psychological state of poverty consciousness (the opposite of prosperity consciousness), and is usually handed down from parent to child. So you, yourself, may never have gone hungry or wanted for anything in your life but because those who brought you up once experienced such hardships, they instilled the same fears in you. Thus, people in America still carry the emotional luggage of fears handed down from the time of the Great Depression of 1929, many in Ireland carry the legacy of the Great Irish Famine of the 1840s, people from many nations remember the rationing of times of war, and so on. By choosing to think differently you can free yourself from the anxieties of those who brought you up, and when you go one step further and focus on abundance rather than worrying about lack, you will happily let go of things you no longer need. In fact you will be eager to let them go to create more space for good things to come to you.

Many books have been written in the last few decades teaching people how to clear patterns of inherited diseases and other family traits. What will happen to your children if you don't learn how to deal with clutteritis yourself? Now is your chance to clean up your family line for all the generations yet to come. And there is a lot of evidence to suggest that such acts not only help those yet to come but can also work back down the spiral of time to help your ancestors retrospectively, which in turns helps you.

A Belief that More is Better

Here's an example. In the west we have a whole selection of culinary knives in our kitchens. We have small knives for chopping small things and big knives for chopping big things; some have pointed blades, some are square-edged; some are lightweight, some are heavy. We carefully select the most appropriate knife for the task in hand. Go to Bali and you will find something interesting. Not only do households only have one knife which can be used for many more purposes than we can imagine, but even a five-year-old child is usually more dextrous with it than most western cooks (just ask one to peel a pineapple for you!). We have been brainwashed by advertising moguls into believing that we need such a range of cutting implements and now most of us have lost the skills to be able to manage without them.

This 'more is better' theme is constantly being touted to us by manufacturers who want to create a need in order to sell their products, and gullible folk fall for it every time. Next time one of those 'useful-gadgets-you-didn't-realise-you-needed' catalogues pops through your letterbox, spend a hilarious half-hour reading it and getting convinced how much better your life would be if you only had a non-slip, multi-purpose, easy-care whatever-it-is, and then toss the brochure gleefully in the recycling bin without ordering. Pulling back from the brink of certain shopping is tremendously empowering, and you never would have used it anyway!

'Scroogeness'

Entrenched clutterholics refuse to let go of their junk until they feel they have really got their money's worth out of it. This applies even if the item was purchased at a bargain price or picked up for nothing. It feels indecent to let it go before every last drop of usefulness has been wrung out of it, even if it means that it sits in the cupboard indefinitely waiting for its time to come.

However, if you are hanging on to things for this reason, you will find that life does not treat you kindly. Good things cannot easily come into your life if you block the flow of energy by persistently clinging to outdated clutter. Relax your hold a little and see what happens.

Using Clutter to Suppress Emotions

Do you feel uncomfortable with too much empty space around you or too much free time? Clutter conveniently fills that space and keeps you busy. But what are you avoiding? Usually it is loneliness, fear of intimacy or some other buried emotion which it feels easier to submerge in clutter than have to cope with. However, it takes a tremendous amount of energy to keep it suppressed. You will be amazed at how your life takes off when you finally face your fears and find yourself. Clearing your clutter is one of the most painless ways to do this because you can do it at your own pace.

Obsessive–Compulsive Disorders

Some people have so much clutter they have what amounts to a serious obsessive–compulsive disorder. If you have reached the stage where you never throw *anything* away because you are so worried you may discover later that you need it, this book will help you to understand your problem and you will also need to seek the professional help of an experienced therapist. I have met people who save every till receipt, every plastic bag, every newspaper and everything else because of the paralysing fear of what could happen if they didn't. Then, instead of being a nurturing place from which they can launch themselves into the world, their home becomes their self-created nightmare.

While clutter clearing is by no means a substitute for appropriate therapy, it can be a vital part of the recovery process on the journey to a happier, obsession-free life. For further insights, read the story of 'Mr More, The Man Who Couldn't Throw Anything Away' in Raeann Dumont's *The Sky Is Falling* (see Bibliography).

7

LETTING GO

The process of clearing clutter is all about letting go. Not just letting go of your belongings – that is only the end result. The most important thing is learning to let go of the fear that keeps you holding on to them after it is time to move them on their way.

'They've Come for the Stereo'

I live half of each year in Bali, Indonesia, and half of each year in the west. I have been doing this for the last eight years, ever since I decided to do it. Sometimes people tell me they wish their lives could be like mine. They imagine that I have pots of money and can do whatever I want but the truth is I started with nothing except an insatiable desire to live in Bali for six months of each year. When they look honestly at their own lives and see what prevents them from doing something they say they really want to do, a lot of it is attachment to possessions. They have set their lives up so that they are not free to do what they really yearn to do.

Stuart Wilde is a man after my own heart. I keep arriving in places in the world and hearing that he was just there a few days before me, so one of these days I hope our paths coincide. He has a chapter in his book, *Infinite Self*, which is a total delight. It is called 'Hold on to Nothing'.

> *'Everything you have is in the care of the God Force. If you come home and the stereo is missing, you can say, "Ah, they've come for the stereo," rather than getting uptight about it. It's just gone back to the God Force. Somebody else has it now. That leaves space for another stereo to come into your life. Or it leaves space for no stereo at all. Now you'll have the silence to meditate and think about who you are and what you want in this life.'*

And if you're looking for something to spend your money on, here's his advice:

> *'The whole function of money is not to have it; its function is to use it. The main reason for generating money is to buy experiences. You want to get to the end of your life with zilch in the bank, and look back and say, "My God, look*

*at this huge pile of experiences," because none of your
memories are ever lost.'*

Just Passing Through

Life is constantly changing. So when something comes into
your life enjoy it, use it well, and when it is time, let it go. It is
that simple. Just because you own something, it doesn't mean
to say that you have to keep it for ever. You are just a temporary custodian of many things as they pass through your life.
You can't, after all, take the contents of your kitchen
cupboards with you when you die, and nor would you want to!

Everything material is merely energy in transition. You
may think you own a house or have money in the bank, but
the fact is you don't even own the body you stand up in. It is
on loan from the planet and, after you are done with it, it will
be automatically recycled and reappear in a different form
without you. You are spirit – glorious, eternal, indestructible
spirit – but your human circumstance is what can best be
described as a transient 'rent-a-body' situation.

Your body is the temporary temple of your soul. What you
keep around you in the extended temple of your home needs
to change with you as you change and grow, so that it reflects
who you are. Particularly if you are engaged in any kind
of self-improvement work, you will need to update your
environment regularly. So get into the habit of leaving a trail
of discarded clutter in your wake, and start to think of it as
a sign of your progression!

Let Go of Fear

People hold on to their clutter because they are afraid to let it go – afraid of the emotions they may experience in the process of sorting through the stuff, afraid they will make a mistake and later regret getting rid of something, afraid they will leave themselves vulnerable, exposed or at risk in some way. Clutter clearing can bring up a lot of 'stuff' to be faced and dealt with, and intuitively everybody knows it.

However the rewards for clutter clearing are well worth it. Love and fear cannot exist in the same space, so everything you are holding on to through fear is blocking you having more love in your life; clearing it allows more love to start pouring in. Fear stops you being who you truly are and doing what you came here to do; clutter clearing brings you greater clarity about your life purpose. Fear suppresses your vital life force energy; releasing clutter helps reconnect you to your own natural vitality. Letting go of clutter leaves you free to be you, which is the greatest gift you can ever give yourself.

PART TWO

IDENTIFYING CLUTTER

8

CLUTTER AND THE FENG SHUI BAGUA

If the previous chapters didn't get you motivated to make a start on clearing your clutter, this one is sure to make an impact.

The Bagua Clutter Check

The Feng Shui bagua is a grid which reveals how the different areas of any building you occupy are connected to specific aspects of your life.

If there is a particular area of your home or workplace which always seems to get cluttered as fast as you unclutter it, look to see which area of the bagua it is located in and check what is happening in that aspect of your life. You will most probably find that this is a part of your life which needs constant attention and keeps snagging up. Our lives and the buildings we occupy are inseparable! So it is wise to be more selective about what you keep in that area in order to bring greater ease and harmony to that aspect of your life.

Storing out-and-out junk anywhere can have a more serious effect. A junk room in your prosperity area, for example, can create financial problems in your life. An accountant who attended one of my workshops decided to put this to the test. His business had slumped and he noticed that in the prosperity area of his office there was a stack of broken mirrors and ornaments. He cleared them out and was astonished to receive not just one but two phone calls within a few days from enquirers who became major new clients. What was even more extraordinary was that these were large corporate businesses who had become exasperated with their existing firm of accountants, had suddenly decided to find a new one through the most unusual route of looking through the Yellow Pages in the phone book, and it just so happened that his accountancy firm was the first name they picked! He was so impressed he came back to take another workshop and to tell us all the story. I have also heard of countless similar successes over the years.

Using the Bagua

An in-depth study of the Feng Shui bagua can take many years and after reading this book you may be interested to

Prosperity	Fame	Relationships
Wealth	Reputation	Love
Abundance	Illumination	Marriage
Elders	Health	Creativity
Family	●	Offspring
Community	Unity	Projects
Knowledge	Career	Helpful friends
Wisdom	Life Path	Compassion
Self-improvement	The Journey	Travel

The Feng Shui Bagua (simplified diagram).

look into it further (see recommended books in the Feng Shui Bagua section of the Bibliography). However, for the purposes of getting you motivated to clear your clutter, I am just going to explain it in very basic terms and with a very basic diagram.

Let's say you want to apply the bagua to your home. Get a sheet of ordinary paper and sketch the plans of your building – just an outline showing all the walls and doorways from a bird's-eye view will do. If you rent space in part of a house, don't draw the whole building, just draw the flat or the room you live in.

Next, turn the sheet of paper until the front entrance to your house, flat or room is parallel to the lower edge of the sheet, as if you are facing towards it and about to step inside. The front entrance is the determining factor in how to position the bagua because this is how energy as well as people enter your home. Here are some examples (see the following pages).

(Special note for the Irish and other extra-friendly communities of the world: if you, your family, your visitors and the postal worker delivering your mail use your back door as your front door, then your back door is the door you use for the purpose of aligning the bagua!)

The next step is to locate the centre of your home so that you can draw the bagua on to the plans and read off from it where each area of your life is located in the building. If the building is square or rectangular, this is easy. You simply draw diagonal lines from each of the corners to determine the centre point and line this centre point up with the centre point of the bagua. Notice from these diagrams how the bagua has an elastic quality and stretches to fill the rectangular shape:

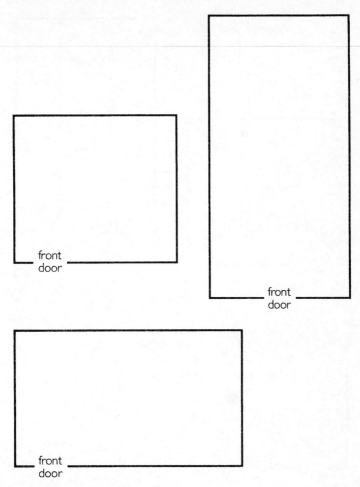

Drawing up a plan of a Regular-shaped building or room.

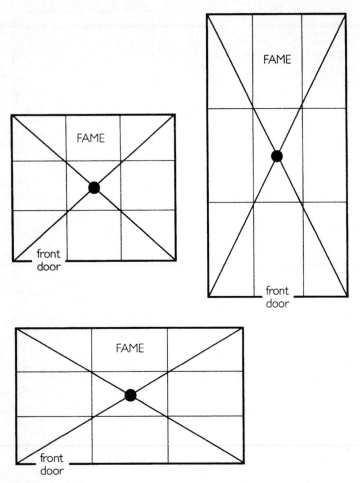

Locate the centre of your home and draw in the bagua.

If the building is an irregular shape, you first have to square it up before you can draw in the diagonal lines to establish the centre point and line it up with the dot in the centre of the bagua (see over).

Baguas Within Baguas

This is where it gets even more interesting. Not only does the bagua apply to the building as a whole, but there is also a larger bagua for the plot of land it stands on (swivel it to align the lower edge of the grid to the main entrance to the plot of land) and a bagua for each room within the building (align the lower edge of the grid parallel to the doorway to each room).

So that puts paid to any ideas you may have had about secretly shifting your junk to a shed at the bottom of the garden. A junk shed in the far left-hand corner of your garden will sabotage your finances, one in the far right-hand corner will put a strain on your relationships, one in the centre of the bottom of your garden can damage your reputation, and so on. There is nowhere you can put clutter where it will not affect you!

Clutter and the Bagua

In my first book, *Creating Sacred Space with Feng Shui*, you will find a wealth of information about creating Feng Shui cures and enhancements in each area of the bagua in order to

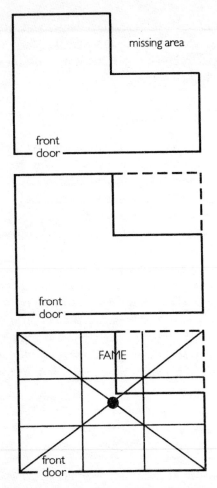

A more complex shape: square off the missing area to locate the centre of your home and draw in the bagua.

improve the corresponding aspects of your life. In this book, my focus is on the effects of keeping clutter in each area.

Try this simple exercise now. Think of a cupboard in your home which is crammed full of stuff – one that has been like this so long that you no longer know what is actually in there. That cupboard corresponds to a part of you. There is a part of you which you have become so out of touch with that you no longer know what is happening in there. To find out what this may be, work out where the cupboard is placed in the bagua for your home and also the bagua for the room it is in. If it is in a room you use a lot, that bagua will be the most important one for your to look at; otherwise, just refer to the bagua of your home as a whole.

The Nine Sections of the Bagua

You will notice that each section of the bagua is described by several different names. This is to give you more of a feel for the different levels and energy frequencies encompassed by each of the areas. Just pick whichever of the names you most resonate with.

Prosperity, Wealth, Abundance, Fortunate Blessings
Clutter in this area will clog up your cash flow, cause your overall financial situation to stagnate and make it hard work to create abundance in your life.

Fame, Reputation, Illumination   When this area is

cluttered it can cause your reputation to dull and your popularity to wane. Enthusiasm, passion and inspiration will also be in short supply.

Relationships, Love, Marriage   A cluttered relationships area can cause difficulty in finding a love mate or problems in an existing relationship. What you get will not be what you need or want.

Elders, Family, Community   This type of clutter can cause problems with superiors, authority figures and parents, as well as within your family or community as a whole.

Health, Unity   Clutter here has damaging health consequences and your life will lack a meaningful central focus.

Creativity, Offspring   If this area is cluttered you are likely to experience blocks in your creativity, struggle in bringing projects to fruition and difficulties in relationships with children or people working for you.

Knowledge, Wisdom, Self-improvement   Clutter in this area limits your ability to learn, make wise decisions and improve yourself.

Career, Life Path, The Journey   When you have clutter here it can seem as though life is an uphill struggle. You feel that you are in a rut, not doing what you want to do – and probably not even knowing what that is.

Helpful Friends, Compassion, Travel   Clutter in this area blocks the flow of support in your life, so you will feel like you are 'going it alone' a lot of the time. It also inhibits plans to travel or move home.

The Bagua Test

I am a great sceptic and I wholeheartedly encourage you to test the validity of this information before accepting it. One way you can do this is to pick one of the areas of the bagua which is going well in your life, drag a whole pile of junk into it, leave it there for a few months and see what happens. I did this once and it was a disaster!

Another more productive way, which I would definitely recommend in preference to the first method, is to pick an area of your life which is *not* going well and do some clutter clearing in the relevant areas of the bagua. For example, supposing you feel generally unsupported. You would need to clear any clutter in the helpful friends area of your garden if you have one, the helpful friends area of the bagua of your home as a whole, and the helpful friends areas of the main rooms you spend time in. If any of these places are inaccessible for any reason (supposing you have a lodger living in that part of your home, or whatever), you will need to do an extra good job in those areas you can get to.

Of course the very best way is to aim to clear *all* your

clutter, wherever it is. This will help all aspects of your life equally well.

The next section of the book is about identifying specific types of clutter, and begins by taking a look at favourite clutter zones where your junk is most likely to accumulate.

9

CLUTTER ZONES IN YOUR HOME

Think of your home as a graphic three-dimensional representation of your own life. If you share the space with others you may like to claim that it represents their lives more than your own, especially if they outnumber you, but you can't get out of it this easily. Everything around you is a reflection of yourself, and this includes not just your home but any other people who live in it too and what they create there.

This chapter looks at some of the primary areas where clutter collects and how they can affect you.

BASEMENTS, ATTICS AND JUNK ROOMS

Basements and Other Types of Under-House Storage

Your basement or cellar symbolises your past and your subconscious mind. A cluttered basement symbolises issues from the past not dealt with, often very weighty issues (people tend to put their heaviest junk in basements). The length of time it has been down there will tell you how long you have been putting off dealing with what is symbolically buried in the stuff – and remember to add the period of time it wasn't being used before it got relegated to the basement.

If you leave things in your cellar long enough, the chances are that mildew, mice, damp, fungus or some other natural saviour will intervene to help you decide to dump it. But while these processes are happening, how are they affecting your life? Feeling hopeless, depressed, lethargic, aimless or burdened in your progress are just some of the unfortunate side-effects subterranean clutter can have.

Of course you can use your cellar for some storage, but you need to regularly review what is there, only keep things you actually use from time to time, and don't have so much stuff down there that air and energy cannot circulate.

Attics

Things stored in your attic can restrict your higher aspirations and possibilities. It is as if you sabotage yourself by creating a false limitation. You will tend to worry more about the future than other people, as if there are problems hanging over you, ready to drop at any time! After clearing out their attics many people write to tell me what a difference it makes:

'It took me a week to clear out the attic but it felt fantastic and I am buzzing with energy.'

'I had over forty years' memorabilia stored in my attic – old love letters, photos, trinkets and souvenirs. They were just gathering dust and entertaining the mice. I cleared the lot and converted my attic to an art studio which has now become my favourite room in the house. My new-found creativity has brought me such joy.'

'I booked a consultation with you because my business had plateaued out several years ago and I was hoping you could work your Feng Shui wonders to move it on to bigger and better things. The last thing I expected you to recommend was to clear out the attic and I must admit I wouldn't have done it if it had been left to me. It was my wife who finally talked me into it and I just want to let you know that it has been exactly as you said – like taking the lid off my

business. It has completely taken off in new and exciting ways, like a dream come true.'

Junk Rooms

Hopefully the chapter on the bagua put you off ever having one of these again. The murky energy that emanates from junk rooms is highly undesirable and can really put a spanner in the works of whichever aspect of your life it is connected to. If your circumstances are such that you absolutely must have a junk room for a while longer, then at least tidy and organise what is in there.

Junk Drawers

What I am about to say may surprise you. My advice is: Do have one. Designate one drawer which you can just throw things into. If you live in a big house, you may even need a junk drawer on every floor.

This whole clutter clearing thing is not about being obsessively perfect – it is about handling your belongings in such a way that the energy of your home is vibrant and flowing rather than dull and stagnating. In our busy world, we sometimes need the blessed relief of just opening a drawer and chucking in all those odd things that are littering the place. So do have a junk drawer but just follow these three rules:

1. Choose a small drawer

2. Use it sparingly
3. Have regular clear-outs.

Entrances, Doorways and Passageways

Your Main Entrance

In Feng Shui, the main entrance to your home represents your approach to the world as you look out, and your approach to your own life as you look in. Just as people enter and leave through this doorway, so, too, does energy. If the area is cluttered in any way it can restrict the flow of opportunities coming to you and hinder your progress in the world. This is a very important area to keep clear. Clutter near the main entrance creates unnecessary struggle in your life.

Next time you use this door, take a long, objective look at what you see. Is the pathway to it cluttered by overhanging branches or overgrown plants? Is there junk outside the door or visible from the pathway as you approach or leave the building? Do you have to fight your way in past pegs of bulging coats hung five deep, scattered shoes, wellyboots, raincoats, hats, gloves, scarves and other assorted paraphernalia? Organise this area so that it is as clutter-free as possible, and especially make sure that there is no clutter wedged behind the door which prevents it from opening fully.

Your Back Door

As you will discover later in this book when I come to talk about the wonders of colon cleansing, everything eats and excretes. If your front door is the mouth through which things enter then it logically follows that your back door is ... (you can figure this out for yourself). So if you don't want your home to be constipated, don't let clutter accumulate here either.

Behind Doors

One very simple way to test whether Feng Shui works or not is to go through your home and clear clutter from behind all your doors. This includes things hanging from hooks and doorknobs (dressing-gowns, towels, bags, you name it), as well as things which obstruct them from opening fully (furniture, laundry baskets, etc.). Then notice how much easier your life becomes. This is so simple and so effective. When your doors cannot open fully, the energy cannot flow freely around your home, so everything you do takes more effort. When you remove the clutter, the energy flows more smoothly and so does your life.

Passageways

Clutter in corridors, passageways and stairways obstructs the flow of life-bringing energy through your home, so your life lumbers rather than jaunts on its way. The worst type is clutter which causes you to contort your body as you go because you have to manoeuvre around it. Keep all these areas as clear as possible.

LIVING AREAS

The Lounge/Sitting Room/Living Room/ Family Room

These vary enormously from home to home. Some are kept fastidiously clean, tidy and clutter-free so that they are always presentable when visitors call. Others look permanently like a hurricane just swept through. The important thing is that your home has a 'heart', where people naturally feel drawn to spend time and 'hang out' with each other. Even if you live alone, there still needs to be a place where you do this with yourself. A house without a heart is not a home.

Sometimes the kitchen table or dining room becomes the gathering point of this energy, or it may be the lounge or family room. Wherever it is, it is important that the energy doesn't whizz through the space too quickly. It needs to be able to collect and blend before moving on its way. So this is one instance where a few well-placed ornaments can be placed to anchor the energy and create a homely atmosphere. Make it as inviting as possible, and it is particularly important to have an attractive centrepiece which symbolises something relevant and inspiring to the people who live there.

The Kitchen

What is lurking in your kitchen cupboards? A man who came to one of my workshops shared with us that after reading my book he decided to eat his way through all the food he had and not go shopping again until he had consumed the lot. He said he managed to live like this for nearly eight weeks! In the end he was down to ten cans of food he didn't like, so he threw them out and went shopping!

Have a major clear-out of all your cupboards, and don't forget your fridge and freezer.

BEDROOMS

Things That Don't Belong in Bedrooms

Is your bedroom a dumping ground for all those things you have nowhere else to put? If so, you are treating yourself like a second-class citizen. It's really not ideal to have computers, exercise bikes, broken-down equipment and other unseemly objects crowded into your sleeping area. Clutter in the bedroom is a real no-no, for children and adults alike.

For those who are romantically inclined, whether you are

single and looking or already in a relationship, it will pay you dividends to keep your bedroom tidy and clutter-free. Stale energy hangs around dirty laundry so never keep a laundry basket in the bedroom, and be sure to change your bedsheets at least once a week to keep your energy vital and fresh. These tips will improve your sleep as well as your love life.

Under Beds

Anything in your energy field affects the quality of your sleep, so resist the temptation to stash junk under your bed. If you have one of those beds that has drawers in it, the best thing you can keep in there is clean bed linen, towels or clothing.

Dressing Table Tops

It is a curious and little-known fact that when people have lots of bottles and containers on dressing table tops, most of them are virtually empty! Check yours and see!

Keep the surfaces in your bedroom as clear as you can so that the energy can move smoothly and harmoniously around the space.

On Top of Wardrobes

Clutter crammed on top of wardrobes and cupboards is like problems hanging over you waiting to be dealt with. It impedes your ability to think clearly and freshly, and if it's the first thing you see when you wake up in the morning, you will tend to wake up sluggishly. Lots of clutter in your home stashed higher than eye level will have a generally oppressive effect, and you may suffer from headaches.

Inside Wardrobes

Most people wear about 20 per cent of their wardrobe 80 per cent of the time. If you doubt me, do this test for a month: each time you wear something and launder it, hang it at one end of your wardrobe. At the end of the month you will find (unless you have deliberately changed your habits to beat this exercise or have a job that requires you to vary your outfits often) you are wearing these same clothes most of the time.

Actually it's not just the clothes you wear that follow this 20/80 pattern. It can be applied to everything else you own and to most activities in life. We all get 80 per cent of our results from 20 per cent of our efforts (this is known in the business world as the Pareto principle, named after an Italian economist who first figured it out). Similarly, we get 80 per cent use from 20 per cent of our belongings.

So when it comes to clearing out your wardrobe, first separate your clothes honestly into the 20 per cent you love to wear and the 80 per cent which are just taking up space, and it becomes much easier to dump the excess.

When sorting through your 80 per cent pile, it is wise to

get clear on your criteria for whether something stays or goes. First check out the colours. A great investment is to have a professional colour consultation to discover which colours uplift and enhance your energy, and which colours do the opposite. You will walk away with a swatch of colour samples that are sure to make you look and feel great, and this does wonders for your self-assurance. This helps you to sift through at least 50 per cent of your clothes and discard them for ever more, because it suddenly becomes abundantly obvious to you that they never did anything for you in the first place.

Next, try on each item in the remaining pile and see how you feel. If you don't like the shape, the texture, the cut, the material or anything else about it, let it go. You owe it to yourself to create a collection of outfits you absolutely love, so that never again do you open a wardrobe bulging with clothes and moan, 'But I've got nothing to wear!'

Make a decision to never, ever buy anything again which isn't quite what you want, because now you know it will just end up in the 80 per cent pile and you will have wasted your money. Resolve to buy only clothes which you love and which look great on you, and if this means that you buy three gorgeous outfits which cost a bit more rather than twenty duff cheaper ones, so be it. And, yes, I recommend you do this even if you are short of money. In fact, making a point of always looking good and feeling good is one of the best ways you can raise your energy and so attract to yourself better prosperity.

Clothes and Energy Vibrations

Some people keep things they haven't worn in over twenty years. They say that if they hang on to them long enough they will come back into fashion. My advice is: if you haven't worn it in the last year, and especially if you haven't worn it in the last two or three years, then let it go. In one year you will have gone through a cycle of all the seasons, and if you haven't felt the urge to wear it in all that time then that particular article of clothing has had its time. If two or three cycles of the seasons have gone by without you wearing it, then it is definitely time to let it go.

It may be useful if you can understand why those clothes will never be appropriate again. In the same way that we decorate the walls of our homes, we choose colours, textures and designs of fabrics that we wear to reflect our own energy vibrations. For example, people go through colour phases. Several years ago my entire wardrobe was purple with a few green, blue and turquoise items, but it was purple I was really big on. Someone came to find me in Bali and knew which house was mine by the sheer quantity of purple laundry hanging out to dry! At that time I was stacking lots of purple energy into my aura, which was to do with reclaiming my own power and prosperity. Now I have integrated the colour and so I hardly ever wear it.

Most people have some items in their wardrobes which they bought, wore once and have never worn again. What happens is that you are out shopping one day and your eye catches on something, let's say it's orange with purple polka dots. You try it on and it looks fantastic (to you) so you buy it. Well, it so happened that on that particular day you were a bit off-balance emotionally and the colours in your aura had changed to orange with purple splodgy bits, or something complementary to those colours, so the new clothes looked great. But by the next day that particular emotional set has dissipated, your aura is back to its usual colours and the clothes don't look so great to you any more (they never did to anyone else!). You wait for the cycle to come round again but usually (mercifully) it's a one-off with few or no repeats. The trick is: never go shopping when you feel emotionally out-of-sorts. Comfort shopping is one sure way to end up with a wardrobe of clothes you will never wear.

Some people hang on to clothes that are too small for them because they are planning to lose weight so that they can wear them again. It rarely happens this way. If this is you, do yourself a favour and take a tip from Denise Linn which I have passed on to many people with tremendous results. Throw all these clothes away, and go out and buy yourself something which makes you look and feel really good exactly as you are now. And guess what usually happens? You lose weight. Call it sod's law if you like, but it works, and the reason is that you have stopped resisting being fat. You have decided to love yourself exactly as you are instead of waiting until you lose weight. What you resist persists, and when you stop resisting, it stops persisting!

BATHROOMS

Some bathrooms I see are stacked to the hilt with appliances and beauty and grooming products. They are on shelves, window-sills, on top of the toilet cistern, round the bath rim, next to the washbasin, on the floor, and anywhere else there is space. This makes it so much more difficult to clean the inevitable gungy deposits they leave and creates a confused, chaotic theme in an area which ideally needs to be calm and peaceful. People with clutter-free bathrooms find some of their meditations (and also their best songs!) happen in their bath-tub or shower. For best results, install some storage units and keep them organised and clean, inside and out.

GARAGES/CAR PORTS

These are a clutterholic's delight, providing a great place to store parts of cars you no longer own, bits of furniture you no longer use, boxes of stuff you never did like, and everything else you can't squeeze into the house. Dedicated hoarders will gladly leave their expensive cars parked outside in all weathers so that their worthless clutter is safe and dry. I even know one family who moved from a house with a garage attached to a house with *two* garages attached, simply because they needed the extra clutter storage space!

Garages *can* be used to keep things in, but only for items

you use and like. A clean, well-organised garage space can be a delight.

Cars

The state of most people's cars is a real give-away as to their true state of clutterdom. If you have cleared the clutter in your home but are driving round knee-deep in rubbish, there's still work to do!

Your car is like a small world unto itself. Do you cringe and apologise for the state of it whenever you give someone a lift? How many times a week do you think to yourself, 'This car really could do with a good clean out'? Every time you think about it, your energy dips, until eventually it is costing you more energy not to do it, than to just roll up your sleeves and get on with it. You know how good it feels when it has been freshly tidied out and valeted. Treat yourself!

PORTABLE CLUTTER

I am talking here about handbags, shoulder bags, briefcases, trouser pockets, and so on. Now just in case you wonder if I walk my talk or just write books telling other people what to do, it happened that just a few days ago I was visiting some friends and their two-year-old child decided it was guest handbag inspection time. Out it all came, piece by piece, while her mother and father looked fondly on. Apparently this little girl ransacked handbags regularly, leaving a trail of embarrassed women in her wake. I can assure you it is a wonderful feeling to sit back and watch with enjoyment rather than concern. Her parents had been prepared to apologise to me but instead they awarded me the prize for the tidiest handbag they had ever seen. Of course it's not always so immaculate, but I really can't see the point of carrying a bag of litter with me everywhere I go, so regular tidy-outs are as fundamental to me as laundering my clothes.

On an International Note

I have noticed that clutter zones vary from country to country. In Australia, as an example, people tend to have garages or storage areas under the house, so this is where they tend to put their clutter. In England, attics and basements are a favourite. In Ireland, they love to fill sheds and outhouses behind the house. And Americans just stash it EVERY-WHERE!

10

COLLECTIONS

Most people collect something. The less imaginative go for thimbles, teaspoons, match boxes, telephone cards, beer mats or stamps while the more eccentric gather deceased pop star memorabilia, antique exhaust pipes, sewing machine attachments, cats' whiskers and the like (yes, I've actually met people who do collect such things). Another favourite is animal ornaments, which have global popularity. Most sought after are cats, dogs, frogs and ducks, with local variations such as kangers and koalas down under, elephants, tigers and dragons for the more orientally inclined, and so on.

Having a few cute kittens on the mantelpiece is one thing, but these collections can get out of control. Soon there are cat ornaments in every room, cat pictures on every wall, cats on your tea-towels, your tee-shirts, your cushions, your coffee cup. I was talking about this subject once at one of my seminars in Southern Ireland. After a while, a woman sitting in the front row could no longer contain herself and burst out with the public confession that she had over 2,000 frog ornaments in her home. 'Even my front door is made of a huge carved frog!' she exclaimed with such pathos that she reduced the audience to hysterical laughter.

Why People Collect Things

So why do we do this? If traced back, some people find that their attraction to what they have chosen to collect began during childhood. For others, it was a gift they received which well-meaning friends and relatives then added to. Whatever the case, when we feel moved to collect a particular type of thing, or even when we 'accidentally' end up with such a collection, what we are in fact doing is responding to an intuitive need to gather a particular type of essence which we need for our own personal growth. It's a specific frequency which we need to bring into ourselves at that time and is entirely valid. But life is constantly changing and moving, and we actually only need to collect that essence for as long as it takes us to spiritually integrate it into our life. Then we can move on to something new.

Where animal essences are concerned, the native Americans knew a great deal about this. Each person was known to have an animal totem, which was both a protection and a source of power and wisdom for them. Members of the tribe would often take names such as 'White Eagle', 'Dancing Bear' and so on, and they would live in close affinity with that essence throughout their lives. But times have changed. Just as in the olden days in England they would call a man 'Jack the Smith' or 'John the Fisher' after his trade (which became abridged to Jack Smith and John Fisher), the speed at which we live has now increased so much that the modern equivalent would be something like 'Richard the Computer Programmer turned Taxi Driver turned Organic Farmer turned Author'. Most people can expect to have several professions in their lifetime, and often several marriages or primary relationships too. It is as if we are now living many lifetimes in the space of one.

The reason for this lies in the unseen worlds of energy. Denise Linn refers to it as the increased 'squiggle rate', meaning the rate at which energy vibrates. The faster it moves, the higher we can reach in the spectrum of human possibility. Therefore the last thing we want to do is get stuck on collecting frogs, when there is a whole world of exciting new possibilities out there just waiting to be tapped!

The Man Who Made Pigs

One man I knew got into making pigs. It all began when his mother bought a plaster pig in a junk shop and he liked it so much he made a mould and copied it. Soon he progressed from plaster pigs to painted porcelain pigs. Then someone suggested he put wings on them to make them more interesting, and thus the flying pig was born. He opened a kitsch market stall in London's fashionable Covent Garden and sold flying pigs by the thousand. He made them in different sizes and people bought them in sets to hang on their walls. At Christmas he made special heaps of sleeping pigs. Looking back he says he had always felt from the start that there was a purpose, some reason why he felt impelled to make them, but it took sixteen years for him to discover what that was and for his passion for pigs to be all played out. He found out that his mother's father and *both* his mother's grandfathers had all been – pork butchers! He estimates that his final total of over 32,000 pigs made roughly equalled the number of pigs his ancestors may have slaughtered in their lifetimes. The karmic debt rebalanced, he closed his stall and moved on to a new life as a shiatsu massage practitioner!

The Duck Woman

In the house of a woman I did a Feng Shui consultation for, I counted over a hundred ducks as she showed me round. 'What's with the ducks?' I asked her, only to be met with a blank stare. 'What ducks?' she asked. We went round again and when I pointed them all out to her she was astonished. They were in her wallpaper, embroidered on her cushions, ornamenting her bathroom, on the front of her nightgown, on her tableware. It was total duckdom but she was completely unaware there were so many. What was even more revealing was that every duck was a solitary one, and the big issue in her life was that she had never married. To cut a long story short, she took my advice, dumped her ducks and found her man!

Don't be a 'Hector the Collector'

The art of understanding collections is to find out why you are doing it, learn from it, and then move on. Don't limit yourself. Make space for something new to come into your life. Don't be a 'Hector the Collector' all your life without ever realising why.

If it's ornaments of the animal kind you find yourself collecting, a good way to discover why you are so attracted to your chosen beastie is to look it up in an animal tarot pack, such as the Medicine Cards (widely available in New Age bookshops). This will give you insights into the qualities you are unconsciously wanting to draw to yourself. It may take a while for you to integrate this information to the point where you genuinely feel ready to let go of your collection and move on, and even then, dumping all your ducks may seem too much to handle in one go. It is very important that you allow this process to happen naturally rather than forcing it, so just gradually trim your flock (or herd etc.) as you feel able.

11

PAPER CLUTTER

What is it about paper that is so attractive? It was predicted that the electronic age would reduce the amount of paper in use but, to everyone's astonishment, we are using more of it than ever before. Here's how to deal with some of the trickiest areas.

Books

Holding on to old books is a very common problem, especially for people with enquiring minds. To many, books are like faithful companions. They are always there to keep you company when you need them, to impart knowledge, inspire, entertain, and stimulate you in a myriad of different ways.

But the problem with holding on to old books is that it doesn't allow you to create space for new ideas and ways of thinking to come into your life. Your books symbolically represent your ideas and beliefs, and when you have too many of them sitting on bookshelves in your home, you become set in your ways and develop fusty energy like the fusty old books you surround yourself with.

Often when I am called in to do a consultation for an educated person who is having difficulty finding a love partner, I find that in the relationships corner of the house or the relationships corner of a much-used room in the house, there is a large bookcase stuffed full of old books. Without knowing anything about Feng Shui they will do this because it 'feels right' there – because in actual fact their primary relationship is with their books! These are the type of people who also have a pile of books by the bed for night-time reading – again, a relationship substitute. By moving the bookcase or at least clearing some space in the bookshelves, it creates room for new interests and relationships in their life.

Maybe you have so many books that they have long outgrown your bookshelves and have taken up residency in other locations. Are they stacked high on your desk, on the coffee table, next to your favourite armchair, or in the loo (see Chapter 18 for the deeper implications of this!)?

Learn to let your books go when it is time. Begin with cookbooks you've never used (no, don't open them and check for recipes!). Move on to text books and reference books you haven't touched in years, children's books you or yours have outgrown, novels you weren't interested enough to begin or finish, books with theories you don't agree with. Progress to volumes that are in such inaccessible places you haven't touched them in decades or are so old they have disintegrated with age. Then there are books which inspired you deeply years ago but whose concepts are now so much a part of you that you no longer need to read them any more. Aim to end up with a collection of books which represents you as you are today and the intended 'you' of tomorrow. Add some reference books that you commonly use, allow yourself the luxury of a few other books simply because you love them or love your associations with them, and let the rest go.

Donating books to the local library is one excellent solution if you are really anxious that you will miss them. It is very comforting to know that if you ever need them, you can borrow them back for a while. In the mean time they are being useful to others instead of clogging up your bookshelves and clogging up your life. The interesting thing about donating books to the local library is that people very, very rarely ever find they want to borrow them back. After letting them go, they move on to something new in their lives and forget all about those old tomes.

Magazines, Newspapers and Clippings

In one house I visited there was a whole room full of aeroplane magazines which had been waiting over twenty years to be sorted so that the owner could discover which issues he was missing to complete the set. When I asked him what he would do when the set was complete, he was dumbfounded. He had to think for a long time to remember why he wanted them. Collecting had become the goal, rather than using them for any purpose. When he gave himself permission to stop collecting and just let them go, he wrote to tell me what a huge relief it had been to take them to the local recycling bin and how wonderful it was to have an extra room in his house so that he could now invite guests to visit!

Another client's study had vanished under a sea of newspapers and magazines she was keeping until she had time to sort through them for articles. There were also three enormous piles of clippings next to her desk which were waiting for further sorting and filing. When I suggested she could dump the lot and give herself a fresh start, panic came into her eyes, as if this could have life-threatening consequences! When we took a minute to look at this objectively together, it came down to her being genuinely afraid that she would inadvertently throw away some article that would prove to be vital to her existence. This is a variation on the 'this-may-come-in-useful-one-day' syndrome, which is based on fear rather than in trusting life to bring to you exactly what you need when you need it.

It is wonderful to want to keep on learning all the days of your life. But we are bombarded today by so much information that we need to be selective. If you want to keep clippings, create a filing system for them and keep it up to date. Have periodic sort-outs and get rid of information which is no longer valid. If you have a pile of clippings waiting to be filed, set yourself a reasonable time period (say, by the end of the month) and, if they ain't filed by then, file 'em in the bin. When you have finished with your magazines, don't hog them. Read them and pass them on to hospitals, dentists, nursing homes, schools and other public places where they can be used, give them to relatives, friends or colleagues who will enjoy them, or just recycle them.

I encouraged this client to sit down and make a list of the many things she wanted to do in her life that she wasn't allowing herself to do because of unfinished jobs such as this. This gave her a completely new perspective with which to review all the tasks she had set herself and it became an easy decision for her to keep just one recent pile of magazines and send the rest on their way. The next time I saw her, the change was remarkable. The greyish gloom which hung around her had disappeared, even the bags under her eyes had all but vanished, and everything about her had become so animated and alive. It seemed she had not stopped with newspaper clippings but had clutter-cleared her entire study and then her entire house. It had totally revitalised her life.

Sentimental Stuff

Some of the nicest letters I receive are from dear, sweet, sentimental souls who collect this type of clutter. Here's one of my favourites:

'I live in South Africa, and have just finished reading your wonderful book on creating sacred space. I wish I could find a way of thanking you for the space you have given me to find a way to use the energies in my home to maximise my joy. Everything you wrote touched a chord inside me, making me aware of the latent thoughts I had about so many things. I have recently thrown away so much junk I have collected over the past thirty years, old love letters, old photos and other bits and pieces I don't know what I was holding onto for. As a consequence, I feel so much better. Lighter in the world. You have found some real wisdom, and bless you for passing it on.'

This category of clutter includes wedding memorabilia, Christmas and birthday cards from years gone by, holiday postcards from friends, personal diaries from the year dot, your children's crayon masterpieces from twenty years ago, and so on. The older you get, the more you have. You rarely look through any of it but you just like to know it is there.

My advice? Keep the best and fling the rest! Keep the ones you really love, which have wonderful, fond associations. Let go of any which you are keeping out of any sense of guilt or obligation, have any ambivalent feelings about or just have too many of.

One woman I met had drawers and drawers full of Christmas and birthday cards that had been sent to her, which she assured me had such sentimental value she could never part with them. But when we sat down and looked through them together, she became sadder and sadder, grieving for the happiness of times gone by. Making the decision to clear them out and start to build her social life afresh marked the beginning of her transformation from the lonely individual she had become to the socially outgoing person she longed to be.

If you have huge quantities of sentimental archives, the first pass is unlikely to be enough. You will probably need to refine the process even further by going through them again at a later date. It will be a constant, ongoing process which may seem hard at first but gets easier every time you do it.

Photos

Do you have drawers or albums stuffed full of photos? Enjoy your photos while they are current. Make colourful montages, put them on the wall, put them in your wallet, stick them on your notebooks, make postcards and send them to your friends. Really get the most from them while their energy is fresh and new. Don't keep photos which remind you of tough times in the past. Just keep the ones which make you feel good and let the rest go. Clear the space for something new and better in your life.

CLEAR YOUR DESK

If you work from home or have a desk you use at home, this next section is for you. The first step is to do one simple sum:

calculate the percentage area of naked desk you can actually see. Don't cheat and tidy your desk before you do this. Just leave it exactly as it is to get an honest appraisal of the situation.

Now, I see hundreds of desks a year in my consultancy work, both in businesses and private homes, and one thing most of them have in common is that there is virtually no space on them where a person can work! Usually there is an area about the size of a piece of paper which has been left free and everything else is occupied, either with equipment or with stacks of paper waiting for attention.

Clear your desk! There's a wonderful book by Declan Tracy with just that title, and in it he describes the desks and business practices of some of the top entrepreneurial business people in the world, who all keep paperwork to a minimum. A clear desk means a clear mind, and a clear mind has vision and perspective. If you are bogged down in paperwork, that's exactly where you'll stay.

Working with a clear desk increases productivity, creativity and job satisfaction. An excellent habit to acquire is to always leave your desk clear whenever you finish working. It is psychologically far more uplifting to start with a clear desk rather than mounds of paperwork, which makes you feel defeated before you even start.

So begin now by removing from your desk absolutely all paperwork which is pending your attention and all objects which are not absolutely vital. I am talking here about only leaving real essentials, such as a computer, a telephone, a pen, a notebook. Keep other extraneous equipment such as staplers, hole punches, paper clips, fluffy toys, bags of munchies and so on on a nearby shelf or in your desk drawer.

Clear Your Disk!

Electronic clutter is just as much a problem as the more tangible variety. Rather than waiting until your hard disk is full to start pruning out programmes and documents you no longer need, a better way is to do a little every day as you go. Go through your files and delete old ones which are cluttering up your hard disk or copy them to an ordered system of disks. Reorganise your filing system within your computer if necessary.

TAKING CONTROL OF PAPERWORK

Here are some tips to help you on your way.

★ Get into the habit of ruthlessly binning (or recycling) as much superfluous paperwork as possible as often as you can.

★ Never jot down messages to yourself on loose pieces of paper. Keep it all in one book and periodically transfer important information to your filing system or computer.

★ Use your noticeboards only for things which are current. If you want to remind yourself to do something, put it in your diary or on a calendar. 'Post-it notes' clutter your mind and make you more likely to forget to do things! Lots of reminder notes dissipate your energy.

★ Bring your financial paperwork up to date and keep it that way. You are far more likely to create prosperity in your life if you become more conscious about dealing with this. Set up systems for paying bills on time, file things where you can find them and love the fact that every bill you receive means you are still credit-worthy! When you learn to pay what you owe with as much joy as receiving what you're due, you will have discovered how to enjoy this money game we humans have created for ourselves rather than getting stressed by it.

★ When you receive a letter, write your reply at the bottom or in the margin and send it back. That way the paper is no longer cluttering up your office, you have saved yourself the time and expense of typing a reply or having it typed, you can do it immediately rather than putting it off for a week, and the person knows they have received your immediate personal attention.

12

MISCELLANEOUS CLUTTER

Clutter certainly comes in all shapes and sizes. Here are some common items often found lurking in the corners and cupboards of many a home...

Things You No Longer Use

★ Outdated leisure equipment (such as games no one ever liked, sports no one plays any more, hobbies you have no interest in now, toys your children have long since outgrown, etc.).

★ Hi-fi equipment you'll never use again (such as speakers to a sound system you no longer own).

★ Keep fit equipment you conscientiously purchased and

never used after the initial inspiration wore off.

★ Health and beauty equipment that's had its day (heated hair rollers, foot massagers, etc.).

★ Spectacles with old prescriptions (several charities can make use of these).

★ Gadgets you purchased to make your life easier, which have turned out to be too much trouble to use.

★ Garden equipment (rusting lawnmowers, tatty garden furniture, old plant pots).

★ Car accessories (roof racks, old tyres, sundry spares).

And so on. I can't even begin to cover the list of strange and curious items people have around their homes and gardens. You can have a good chuckle to yourself as you come across your own.

If you have particularly fond attachments to items which date back to your tender childhood years, here's something you can do which many people have found very liberating – photograph them for posterity and then let them go. The photos will retain those heart-warming images for ever and can be stored in a fraction of the space the items themselves would take up.

Unwanted Gifts

This can be a very sensitive issue for many people. However, here's my very best advice on what to do with unwanted presents: get rid of them. Here's why. Things you really love have a strong, vibrant energy field around them, whereas unwanted presents have uneasy, conflicting energies attached to them which drain you rather than energise you. They actually create an energetic gloom in your home.

The very thought of giving them the elbow is horrifying to some people. 'But what about when Aunt Jane comes to visit and that expensive ornament she gave us isn't on the mantel-piece?' Whose mantelpiece is it anyway? If you love the ornament, fine, but if you keep it in your home out of fear and obligation, you are giving your power away. Every time you walk into the room and see that object, your energy levels drop.

And don't think that 'out-of-sight, out-of-mind' will work. You can't keep that ornament in the cupboard and just bring it out when Aunt Jane is due to visit. Your subconscious mind still knows you have it on the premises. If you have enough of these unwanted presents around you, your energy network looks like a sieve, with vitality running out all over the place.

Remember, it's the thought that counts. You can appreciate being given the gift without necessarily having to keep it. Try adopting a whole different philosophy about presents. When you give something to someone, give it with love and let it go. Allow the recipient complete freedom to do whatever they want with it. If the thing they can most usefully do is put it straight in the bin or give it to someone else, fine (you wouldn't want them to clutter up their space with unwanted presents would you?). Give others this freedom and you will begin to experience more freedom in your own life too.

Things You Don't Like

These are things you bought yourself, but you've never really liked them since the day you got them. Usually you are keeping them until you have the time or money to buy something better.

I'll give you an example. I've never liked ironing very much. I had a perfectly good, average kind of iron but it inspired me not one jot to want to use it. I went to great lengths to make sure I hardly ever wore anything which needed pressing. Then one day, while staying at a friend's house, I discovered what I can only describe as 'the empress of irons'. True, it cost twice as much as the bog-standard item I had at home, but what a joy to use. It took ironing to whole new dimensions I never knew existed. When I got home I went straight out and bought one, then spent a whole afternoon contentedly ironing my way through my wardrobe. For the first time in my life I experienced ironing as a pleasure.

Don't put up with giving yourself second-best. When you nourish yourself by giving yourself the best you can, that signal goes out and will attract the best in other areas of your life too. If you are struggling financially and are just 'getting by' with most of the things you own, love them, be grateful for what you have, and intend that you soon create the resources to replace them with things which inspire you more. Most people are surprised how quickly this becomes possible once they set their mind to it.

Things Which Need Fixing

Things which need fixing are an energy drain. This is because energetically everything you own comes under the mantle of your care and protection. You may conveniently put off doing anything about it but your subconscious mind keeps track of these things, and every time you see the object or one which reminds you of it, your energy drops.

Supposing you have a chair with a wonky leg. You have long since tuned out consciously seeing it when you walk into the room but your eyes *do* still see it, your subconscious mind *does* still register it, and your body never fails to react energetically. When you promise yourself you will repair something and then do not do it, you lose even more power and vitality from your body.

One woman I know lives in a big house where just about everything in it needs fixing in some way. She does admittedly live on a low income with a child to support, but she is a resourceful, capable woman who could fix things if she wanted to. The lack of care and respect that she has for her home reflects the lack of care and respect she has for herself. When you care for your home by looking after it, you are also loving and respecting yourself.

Think of fixing things and improving things in your home as being an investment in yourself. And if there is something you can't be bothered to fix, then get rid of it, or find it a new home with someone who would like it and is willing to repair it.

Double Trouble

I once did a consultation for a clutterholic single woman whose even more clutterholic parents had died and left her everything they had in their home. So she had two kettles, two sets of cutlery, two sets of crockery, two of everything all crammed into her house. In fact, she had three or four of some things. And there just wasn't room. However, she couldn't bring herself to throw anything away because most of the items still had years of use in them. Her home became so energetically clogged that it was literally difficult to breathe in there and her whole life ground to a standstill while she continued the arduous task of sorting through the crates of household items and personal belongings.

Check through your cupboards and count how many of each type of thing you are hoarding. If you have space, fine, but if not, it's time to do some thinning out.

Inherited Clutter

Whoever gave it to you is now in spirit, where there is no attachment to the material world and no clutter! They will understand your need to let it go. If you don't love it or it isn't useful, let someone else inherit it from you now.

Clutter of the Audio-Video Kind

I recently did a consultation for a woman whose kitchen counter was piled high with music cassettes, half of which she admitted she hadn't listen to in the last 10 years. I suggested she could therefore clear 50 per cent of them out and have more kitchen space. 'Wonderful!' she said. 'I'll put them in the attic straight away!'

Of course that wasn't what I had meant! It took a while for her to finally get my reasoning that if she hadn't listened to them in the last 10 years, then she didn't need to hoard them in the attic for another 10 years. Nor did she need to set herself the impossible task of listening to each of them to check that she didn't want to listen to them again! She could just let them go.

Other types of sound and video recordings can be sorted through in the same way, keeping the best and dumping the rest. Everything has its time and then you move on to something new. Keep your audio/video collections current with who you are and what vitalizes you today.

Mystery Items

Everyone has a few of these, especially in the junk drawer. This category includes unidentifiable spare parts you have kept for years, wall-mounting brackets for pieces of equipment you will never mount or no longer own anyway, strange drogits and rubber thingummies which fell off something but you don't know what, and the list goes on. All are prime candidates for clutter clearing.

Boxes

I'll never forget the surprised look on the face of a removal man as he bent to lift one of my large boxes which he expected to be as heavy as all the other ones he had been lifting all morning – and toppled over on his back. That was in the days when I was still a secret hoarder of empty boxes!

My astrological sign is Cancer and we crabs find boxes immensely satisfying and reassuring. Often I am more delighted by the box a present comes in than the present itself! But this can be a very space-consuming passion, and in terms of the Feng Shui bagua, it is not exactly energising to have 'empty box' energy concentrated in any part of the home. I now strictly limit the number of boxes I have and make sure that most of them are put to good use rather than idling empty about the place.

When you purchase new equipment, keep the box it came in for the duration of the warranty period and then trash it. Don't keep the box for ever 'just in case' you move house and need the box to pack it in. It is perfectly easy to pack equipment in standard removal boxes if and when you move house. Another useful tip if you have to store boxes for any reason is to open them out and store them flat. They take up far less space this way and don't have that 'empty' energy any more!

13

THE BIG STUFF

While you are clutter clearing, don't forget the BIG stuff – that horrible old sideboard you have always hated, the grand piano clogging up the living room, the waterbed you never use, the car rusting in your back yard, the tatty twenty-year-old Swiss cheese plant gathering dust in the corner.

Some of these things are so big and moving them is such a challenge that you learn the art of seeing through them as if they no longer exist. You may be able to do this indefinitely but, like it or not, the bigger they are, the more they clog your energy flow and the more important it is to get them off the premises. It is even more important if their symbolism is actively impeding your progress in life. A rusting car in the prosperity area of your garden is sure to affect your finances;

a battered-looking plant in your career area will make you feel tired and lethargic about your work or your life; useless furniture in any area of your bagua will create obstacles in that area of your life; and so on.

Maybe it's not that you have accumulated oversize junk so much as that your home is simply too small to accommodate what you have tried to cram in there. This is often the case if you moved from a large home to a smaller one and have tried to bring all your furniture with you. Or if you have accepted gifts of furniture or collected things which you are keeping until you move to a bigger place. In these cases you need to have a realistic think-up and a practical trim-down. When your home is so full of stuff that there is virtually no room for people you will feel that your life is dictating what you can do. Clearing some space will allow new opportunities to blossom.

Sit down with the ad section in your local newspaper or the Yellow Pages of your telephone directory, and you'll probably find someone who'll be delighted to come and take these outsize items away – and possibly even pay you some money for the privilege. Failing that you may need to pay the council to dispose of them, or get your friends and family to help you dismantle them and take them to the rubbish tip.

Once they are gone, you'll be delighted at the difference and wonder how you ever lived with them for all those years!

14

OTHER PEOPLE'S CLUTTER

You can take a lot of liberties with family, friends and colleagues, but just lay a finger on their clutter and you will soon see some sparks fly! One of the questions I am most frequently asked is what to do about other people's clutter, and especially the clutter of people you live with.

CLUTTER HOARDED BY A PARTNER

Merely discussing your partner's clutter with them can quickly bring to the surface issues that have long been buried in a relationship. Nagging, arguing, threatening and issuing ultimatums only makes clutterholics more entrenched, and

NEVER, EVER, EVER clear their clutter for them unless they specifically ask you to. People have deep emotional attachments to their junk and can get very upset or angry if it is tampered with.

Understand that you can never change anyone else. The only person you can ever change is yourself. In all the years I have been teaching this material, there are only two remedies I have consistently found to be effective in dealing with other people's clutter. They are as follows.

Education

People have to really understand the downside of clutter if they are to have any incentive to do something about it. This is why the same people often reappear at my seminars several months later with a partner in tow, specifically for that person to hear what I have to say. Part of my reason for writing this book is to reach more of these partners without them having to be dragged to my seminars!

Leading By Example

I have heard from a significant number of people that as soon as they started clearing their own clutter, members of their family and close friends, without any prompting from them, suddenly take it into their heads to do the same. In many instances there isn't even any verbal communication between them. Somehow the message goes down the wire to the people they are on the closest frequency to, even if they live at a distance.

One memorable story was told to me by a woman who had read my book and enthusiastically began clutter clearing her home. The process took her the better part of two weeks. During that time, her grandfather, whom she hadn't been in contact with for a while and who lived over two hundred miles away, stunned his entire family by unexpectedly clearing out forty years of junk from his garden shed.

Another woman took a weekend seminar with me in London. While she was sitting in the workshop getting this information about clearing clutter, her husband spontaneously decided to have a huge clear-out and spent the whole day carting six car-loads of clutter to the rubbish tip.

Gemma Massey, who is the first Space Clearing practitioner I ever trained, once gave me a wonderful insight into clutter issues between partners. She naturally lives a very tidy and clutter-free life, and her husband's ever-messy desk really started to bug her. She knew that because it was in her life it must somehow be reflecting a part of herself but, try as she might, she couldn't figure out how that could be. Then one day she suddenly got it. She realised that although her husband is messy on the outside, he is very ordered and organised on the inside; she, on the other hand, is ordered on the outside but not as organised on the inside. And then what happened? Soon after she had had this realisation and started to get more organised inside, her husband spontaneously decided it was time to tidy up his desk and keep it that way!

CHILDREN'S CLUTTER

Where does it all come from? Children's clutter seems to breed and take over space at an alarming rate if it is not checked and controlled!

One of the most important things to instil in a child is confidence. When a child feels loved, secure and happy, they don't have such a reliance on 'things'. Empower them by teaching them clutter-consciousness at an early age so they don't become the clutterholics of the future.

Start by teaching your children to tidy up after themselves. When they get a new toy, decide together where its storage place will be so that they know exactly where to put it away when they tidy up. Periodically get them to make decisions about toys they have outgrown – which to keep and which to give away. Let them make the final decision, though. Something which may look to you as if it had died and gone to heaven may still have huge importance and years of usefulness for your child.

If your offspring seem untamable, realise that all children act out the subconscious minds of their parents, so if you find yourself repetitively nagging them, you will get better results if you work on your own clutter issues first.

TEENAGERS AND CLUTTER

With all those hormones rocketing around in their bodies,

it's understandable that keeping their rooms tidy or clutter-free isn't exactly high on the list of adolescent priorities. Unless they have already got into the way of living clutter-light when they were younger, they probably feel they have quite enough to cope with, thank you very much. Teenage clutter and chaos is usually their inner turmoil showing up on the outside.

I once appeared on a phone-in on a music show on MTV, answering questions from young people about how to use Feng Shui in their lives. The three main topics they wanted help with turned out to be passing exams, making friends, and getting their parents off their case! Most teenagers feel the need for emotional and physical privacy to a greater or lesser degree, and parents need to respect this, just as teenagers also need to respect their parents' space. However, it is reasonable to make an agreement that teenage clutter and chaos is at least confined to specific rooms, and they have regular tidy-ups and clear-outs.

CLUTTER BELONGING TO FRIENDS AND RELATIONS

Sometimes people don't have much clutter of their own but they agree to look after things for friends, neighbours and relatives. 'Please look after this sofa for me while I visit New Zealand.' Two years later you are still waiting for your friend to come back and the sofa has started to grow roots!

Think carefully before you agree to clutter your own space, and if you decide to do it, at least put a time limit on it: 'OK, I'll look after your sofa, but if you're not back for it within X months, it's firewood/will be used to stuff a thousand cushions for Oxfam/or whatever'. Make a clear agreement what will happen to the sofa, and that way your friendship won't deteriorate if things don't go according to plan.

An Australian friend recently told me how she stored her belongings for years while living abroad, paid $700 to move them during that time, and eventually made $60 from selling the lot. Realising that most of the things people ask you to look after aren't worth the boxes they're stored in makes it a whole lot easier not to feel so bad about turning down their pleas for dumping space.

15

CLUTTER AND FENG SHUI SYMBOLOGY

One of the greatest incentives for getting rid of clutter is understanding that keeping the stuff is doing you no good at all. There are two ways that the symbology of the things in your home can affect you. The first is to do with the personal associations you have with something, and the second is to do with the frequency emitted by the object itself.

Personal Associations

If you have things in your home that have unfortunate associations for you, it doesn't matter if they still have years of serviceable life in them, they are cluttering your space and cluttering your psyche.

I once had a boyfriend who would kick things when he got moody, and one day my portable tape deck got the boot. The relationship didn't last long but I kept the tape deck. Every time I used it I saw the damaged bit on top and remembered the incident which had caused it, but I kept it because it was still perfectly good otherwise. This went on for about a year until one day I looked at the tape deck, remembered the incident, and decided I didn't want to be reminded of it ever again. I realised that it had become symbolically associated in my mind with being disappointed by the behaviour of men.

I went straight out, bought a new tape deck, and gave the old one to a girlfriend who needed one. She was very happy. She had no idea why there was a bit of plastic missing off the top and didn't care at all because a slightly imperfect tape deck was a whole lot better than no tape deck at all. For me, however, the negative association I had with it caused my energy to sink every time I saw it, and it was a huge relief to be rid of it.

Outdated Associations

Sometimes the personal associations are not negative but just outdated. For example, when I am called in to do a consultation for someone who is wanting to create a new relationship, I go around the home and often discover many things which belonged to, were gifts from, or still remind the person of a previous partner they haven't quite let go of. Whether they are conscious of the association or not, their energy is constantly being tugged back to the past, and this makes it very difficult to create anything new.

If, say, 50 per cent of your furniture and belongings are associated with a time in your life you want to move on from, then 50 per cent of your energy is tied to the past rather than available in present time. Try as you might, progress will be slow. Similarly, if your home is full of furniture, ornaments or other items which constantly remind you of relatives or friends you have or had difficult or uneasy relationships with, these associations will have an equally draining effect on you.

This also explains why you owe it to yourself to start any important new relationship in a place where neither of you has lived before. The odds are stacked against you when you live in a place where either of you has old associations.

A deep and thorough Space Clearing (see 'The 21 Steps to Basic Space Clearing' at the back of this book) will clear out the old vibrations from your belongings but can do nothing about the mental and emotional associations which are triggered when you see things. One way to deal with this is to spend time and energy forging new, stronger, happier and more positive connections until you reach the point where you completely overwrite and unplug from the old associations. One woman I know painted all the Victorian furniture she had inherited from her grandmother bright blue and yellow to blend in with the rest of her decor, and that did the trick! As she painted, she actively infused the furniture with all the love and joy she could muster, and from that point on whenever she looked at it, that was the strongest association for her.

The other way to do it is dump the lot and start again, and twice in my life I have done this. Both times it was a very scary, yet incredibly refreshing, regenerative experience; a real turning point in my life. My life called for it, but most people don't need to be so radical. Just gradually aim to replace the items you have the most unproductive associations with as you are able.

Frequencies

I have long had the ability to stand in front of a picture and feel its effect. Recently I came across a book called *Life Energy and The Emotions* by John Diamond, in which he explained to me how I do this! For example, he shows an unusual photograph of Winston Churchill with a particular expression on his face and the caption says 'Most people will test weak for the liver meridian when looking at this photo'. Another photograph of someone else is captioned, 'Most people will test weak for the heart meridian when looking at this photo.' and so on, through all the meridians. He has worked out the negative and positive emotional states associated with each of the energy channels in our bodies.

Chinese medicine teaches us that we have twelve pairs of meridians through which energy moves around our bodies, and acupuncture is based on harmonising and rebalancing the flow of energy in these meridians to revitalise the relevant organs they are connected to. John Diamond's research concludes that the function of these energy channels, and thus our general state of health, is very much influenced by positive and negative emotional states. The liver is weakened if you feel unhappy and strengthened when you switch to feeling cheerful; the heart meridian is weakened by anger and strengthened by love and forgiveness; the spleen is weakened by anxiety about the future and strengthened by an attitude of faith in the future; and so on. It is a fascinating study and the book is well worth a read.

What really grabbed me about it, though, was its application to Feng Shui. Many's the consultation I have been on where I have found, in a prominent position in someone's home, a picture, photograph, painting, poster, statue, ornament or other object which is emitting a frequency totally counterproductive to everything the client has told me they want. One woman had a huge, mournful portrait of herself, painted in dark sombre colours, positioned in the most dominant position in her sitting room, next to the doorway which led to the kitchen. She must have seen that portrait a hundred times a day, and I knew immediately from the way it affected my body that she must be depressed. It had cost her so much money she was reluctant to get rid of it, so I persuaded her at least to take it down for a month or so and see how that felt. She was astonished at how much better she felt without it and never hung it up again.

The photos of myself on the back cover of this book and my first book will raise your energy when you look at them.

They were specially produced with this in mind, and the feedback I have had from people of many different cultural, religious and social backgrounds confirms this. They all say to me, 'I just looked at your photograph and knew I wanted to know more about what you do'. This type of Feng Shui symbology is universal in its application.

Arranging Your Home For Symbolic Effect

Now you need to go around your home, look at all your belongings, and ask yourself, 'What is this saying symbolically? How is it affecting me energetically? Is it creating the effect I want or could I do better?'

Begin by culling things which pull your energy down, such as a predominance of downward-hanging things (plants, ornaments, etc.). This is particularly important if you have low-ceilinged rooms, where your energy is squashed before you even begin.

Next, start counting. Do you have things arranged singly, in pairs or in groups? If all your ornaments are solitary, life will tend to dish you up solitary experiences. If you'd rather be partnered, tweak the energy of your home by arranging things in pairs. Happily married people naturally buy two of everything because it feels right (ask some and see!). At first, it will feel strange to you to do this if you have been used to being solitary. You will need to keep doing this until it feels like second nature to you, which will create the shift in your own personal energy field you are looking for.

Another way you can look at the symbology of your home is in the context of the Feng Shui bagua. Check that each area of your home, and each area of each room of your home, has appropriate symbology which supports you in what you want to do in your life.

I remember one client who told me she was always arguing with her employer, and there in the career area of her home was a huge oil painting of a battle scene. Another woman noticed that the prosperity corner of her bedroom was very empty so she went out and bought herself a bouquet of the most abundant-looking flowers she could find for the spot. Her husband arrived home later and for the first time in their twenty-year marriage spontaneously gave her a gift of £1,000 to spend on anything she pleased!

Start to look at everything in your home and ask yourself, 'What does this symbolise to me and how does it make me feel?' The detailed explanation of how to clear clutter in the next chapter will help you sort through your belongings much more easily.

PART THREE

CLEARING CLUTTER

16

HOW TO CLEAR YOUR CLUTTER

Here are three tried and tested ways to deal with your clutter:

1. **The Let-Nature-Take-Its-Course method (also known as the Abdicating-Decision-Making technique)** Put it in a place where it will disintegrate to such a point that you no longer want to keep it. One man I met who was on holiday in Bali confided, 'I cleared out a lot of clutter and put the rest in an outdoor shed. I am hoping that by the time I get back home it will be so mildewed I will have to chuck it out.'

2. **The Wait-Until-You-Die-And-Let-Your-Relatives**

-Sort-It-Out method   This has been a great favourite throughout the centuries. You can even draw up a will telling people exactly what to do with it all!

3. **Take responsibility for the stuff and clear it your-self**   This is the method I recommend. It is far more empowering, has much better karma and allows you to get on with your life immediately, instead of waiting for you or your clutter to expire!

GETTING STARTED

Without doubt, the hardest part is actually overcoming your inertia enough to get started. Once you have begun, the process itself releases more energy to enable you to continue. All the stagnant energy that is locked up in the clutter gets released for you to use in more positive ways. And, the more you clear clutter, the easier it becomes because you know how good it feels after you have done it and you know the positive benefits which follow.

My general rule of thumb is that if I were moving house tomorrow and I would end up with more than one or two rubbish bags full of stuff to throw away, I've got some sorting to do *right now*. I live like this because my life works so much better. It is not a discipline I have to practise – it just makes so much sense to me that I wouldn't want to live any other way. And it isn't something I am fanatical about – I just put a bit of time into it on a regular basis so that everything stays manageable.

So here are some pointers to get you started on The Great Clutter Clear-Out!

Doing it Fast or Slow

People have different amounts and types of clutter, not to mention different levels of willingness to let it go. I find that everyone approaches clutter clearing in one of two ways. One type of person will read this book, cancel all appointments, and ninja through their home like a white tornado, decluttering with glee; the other type does it in stages.

If you need more time, just accept that you do. It may be that you are too busy, too stressed, or just too overwhelmed by the sheer amount of your clutter. Just progress at your own speed, whatever that may be, and do a bit at a time as you feel able. However, bear in mind the following:

If you are busy – remember you DO somehow find the time to acquire the clutter so you CAN make time to get rid of it!

If you are stressed – know that clutter clearing is one of the best therapies there is for worry, stress and anxiety.

If you feel overwhelmed – you won't be if you follow these easy steps, which have already helped thousands of people lighten their load, including many who are far more entrenched clutterholics than you.

The Best Time to Clear Clutter

Any time is a good time. Since most clutter clearing is done indoors, you can do it day or night, any time of the year, come rain or come shine. However, if you happen to be reading this book in spring, this will get you off to a good start. There is a natural instinct to have a good clear-out at this time of the year, when there is new growth and emergence in nature. If you live in a part of the world where there are only two seasons (wet and dry) rather than four, you will find it easier to have a clear-out at the beginning of either of these periods.

Another good time is just after you get back from a holiday. You have a different perspective at these times and it becomes easier to make decisions about what you realistically need to keep. The same is true when you move home, recover from an illness, start a new job, a new relationship or a new era of your life in some other way. But don't make waiting for one of the above to happen an excuse for not beginning. I repeat, any time is a good time!

Most people find they have favourite times of day for clutter clearing. Mine is first thing in the morning. Discover when you are at your most decisive and do your clearing then.

I generally recommend at least one major review of clutter every year, and if you really want your life to work well then it needs to be under constant review. Clear the bulk of it first and then keep it manageable ever after.

Space Clearing to Help Clutter Clearing

It is intended that the information in this book will so motivate you to clear your clutter that it will be all you need. However, if you have read my first book or would like to go deeper into Feng Shui, it may be useful for you to know that doing a full Space Clearing ceremony will help you enormously to get started on clearing the clutter (see 'The 21 Steps to Basic Space Clearing' on page 184). It is ideal if you can do the clutter clearing first, but if you have serious amounts of work to do in this department just skip that part of the Space Clearing preparations and do the rest of the ceremony straight away, just to get the energy in the space moving. Later, after you have cleared the clutter, you can do a Space Clearing ceremony again to re-consecrate the space.

Handling Your Thoughts and Emotions

This book is not telling you that you 'should' do this or 'should' do that but it explains how keeping clutter can affect you so that you can make your own informed choice about it from here on in.

'Should' is one of the most disempowering words there is. When you use it you feel guilty and obligated. My advice is to dump the word from your vocabulary forever and use the word 'could' instead.

Feel the difference: 'I *should* start clearing my clutter today' or 'I *could* start clearing my clutter today'. 'Could' empowers you, gives you choice and later allows you to take the credit for a job well done. 'Should' depresses you, makes you feel at fault and brings you little joy on completion of the task.

I suggest you also dump 'can't' and substitute 'won't'. Then you'll really make some progress. Again, feel the difference: 'I *can't* decide whether to keep this or let it go' or 'I *won't* decide whether to keep this or let it go'. In the 'can't' example, you are helpless and hopeless. In the 'won't' example, you are expressing your decision as a being of free choice, and if you then ask yourself why you won't let it go, you will discover it comes down to some subconscious block you never realised you had 'I won't decide whether to keep this or let it go because it brings up all the feelings to do with my mother/father/spouse ...' and so on. Well, there's still work for you to do but at least you are being honest now.

Make a List

First, take a tour of your home with notepad and pen in hand, noting down the clutter zones in each room. If you are not at home (or are lazy!), just close your eyes and visualise yourself walking from room to room. You will find you know exactly where your clutter is.

Then take another piece of paper and rewrite the list, beginning with smaller clutter zones at the top and working your way down to monster mounds. Examples of smaller zones are behind doors, individual drawers, the bathroom cabinet, small cupboards, handbags, briefcases, toolboxes. Middle-sized zones are wardrobes, kitchen cupboards, linen cupboards, desks, filing cabinets and so on. Large zones are junk rooms, cellars, attics, garden sheds, garages and any clutter-filled spaces that are clearly going to take a while to conquer.

Now put an asterisk beside the zones that irritate you the most. These are the ones to begin with, starting from small to large. Get some small successes under your belt first, and then you will be inspired and encouraged to tackle the bigger areas later. And when you feel how good it feels to tackle the clutter zones that really bug you, you'll be more motivated to wade into those bastions where you wish the clutter would just melt away of its own accord.

Motivating Yourself

Another strong motivator is to use the Feng Shui bagua (see Chapter 8) to check which areas of your life you have been sabotaging by piling junk in that area of your home. Most people are amazed to discover how accurate this system is. Then give some thought to how you would like these aspects of your life to be in the future. Bearing this in mind really helps to get you started and keep at it until the job is done.

Final Preparations

By now you will have some idea how much clutter you are intending to clear so you must create some means of getting it off your premises. Unless you have already decided to order a skip and go for it big time, then simply get some cardboard boxes and/or dustbin bags at the ready. These will be your little army of helpers.

If you decide to use boxes, the basic four you will need are as follows:

★ A **RUBBISH** box
For out-and-out junk, destined for the rubbish tip.

★ A **REPAIRS** box
For items which need repairing, altering, renovating, etc. Only put in here things you are sure you want and need, and set yourself a time limit for getting them repaired.

★ A **RECYCLING** box
For things to be recycled, sold, exchanged, given to someone else, etc. Release them back into the world so that someone else can use them.

★ A **TRANSIT** box
For things which are on their way to somewhere else in your home (to another room, or to a space which hasn't yet been created for them because you need to clear the clutter there first!).

Until you gain experience at this, you will probably also need a fifth box:

★ A **DILEMMA** box
For things you are still in a bit of a dither about whether to keep or let go of.

As the job progresses, you may also feel the need to create sub-divisions of the **RECYCLING** box, such as:

★ A **GIFT** box   For things you have decided to give to friends or relatives.
★ A **CHARITY** box   For things to be donated to charities, libraries, schools, hospitals, etc.
★ A **RETURNS** box   For things to be given back to the people they belong to.
★ A **SELLING** box   For things you can sell or exchange for something you want.

And boxes for each type of thing to be recycled (paper, bottles, etc.).

THE GREAT CLUTTER-CLEAR BEGINS

Begin Small

Choose one small area to clear first. A drawer or small

cupboard is ideal. Give yourself the satisfaction of crossing it off your list when you have done it. Most people find they feel pretty good after doing one area, so they decide to do another, and maybe another. Each small area you clear releases energy for you to do more. Take it at your own pace, doing as much as you feel inspired to do at any one time. This may take you a few hours, a few days, a few weeks or a few months, depending on how much you have to clear and how 'gung ho' you are to clear it. Remember – the speed at which the positive changes will appear in your life is relative to the gusto and decisiveness with which your clutter is cleared!

Larger Areas

When you have tackled some of the smaller areas, start on the middle-sized ones and finally the largest ones, but still break each area down into bite-sized manageable chunks. Divide cupboards into separate sections and rooms into separate areas. You can work through your entire home in this way and gain confidence as you go.

Sorting Through Your Stuff

When you are sorting through things, do *not* create a pile of objects with the intention of deciding later where they will go! Pick up each object in turn and make a decision about it then and there. Does it stay or does it go? If it goes, put it in the **Rubbish** box or the relevant **Recycling** box. If it stays, but is in need of attention, put it in the **Repairs** box. For all the remaining items, decide where they are going to live and go and put them there straight away or put them in the **Transit** box. The **Transit** box is usually the safer option because then there is less risk of your getting sidetracked on your travels. Towards the end of each clutter clearing session you do, take your **Transit** box on a walkabout around your home and relocate its contents in the places you have decided each item will live. If any of these places are already full because you haven't clutter cleared them yet, the items will need to stay in the **Transit** box for a while, which is not ideal, but may be the best you can do.

Make this whole process fun for yourself. Decide now that everything that takes up space in your home has to have a valid purpose for being there. Ask yourself, 'Does it pass the clutter test?'

The Clutter Test

1. Does it lift my energy when I think about it or look at it?

2. Do I absolutely love it?

3. Is it genuinely useful?

If the answer is not a resounding 'yes' to question 1, and an equally resounding 'yes' to either question 2 or 3, then what is it doing in your life?

1. **Does it lift my energy when I think about it or look at it?**

   Recognising whether you feel energised or not is the most reliable part of the clutter test. Your mind can fool around with you and invent all kinds of excuses so that you get to hang on to stuff, but your body knows the truth and never lies. Trust the feeling in your body.

2. **Do I absolutely love it?**

   If so, does it really inspire me or is it just 'nice'?

   Do I already have enough of this type of item for my needs?

   In spite of how much I love it, does it also have sad associations in my life?

3. **Is it genuinely useful?**

   If so, when did I actually last use it?

   When, realistically, am I likely to use it again?

It's Safe to Let Go

Affirm to yourself as you sort through your things, 'It's safe to let go'. Clearing clutter is about letting go and trusting the process of life to bring you what you need when you need it. Anything you are keeping 'just in case', you are keeping through fear.

If you have a lot of clutter, you may need to go through it several times before you feel ready to let go of some things. In some cases, it may take a whole year or more before you finally admit to yourself that it still hasn't come in useful for anything!

There are no Wrong Choices

Like learning anything else in the world, clutter clearing is a skill which you can develop. You can think of yourself as needing to build your clutter clearing 'muscle'. The more of it you do, the more proficient you become and the easier it gets, but when you first begin you can feel like a clutter clearing weakling.

Many people put off having a clear-out because they worry so much that they will get rid of something and really regret it later. After you have been doing it for a while you will come to realise that there are no wrong choices, ever. Even if you regret throwing something away, you can trust that for some reason your Higher Self led you to make that decision and in time you can come to know why it was best for it to happen. I actually believe this applies not just to clutter but to everything in life. Every choice you make is a right choice. What is really important is not the choice, but the reason why you make it. Any choice made from fear is a disempowering choice.

The Dilemma Box

While you are learning the knack of making more empowering choices, you may need to use the **Dilemma** box. When you come across things which you know really do constitute clutter but in your heart you do not feel ready to part with them yet, put them in the **Dilemma** box and then stash the box away in the deepest, darkest recess of one of your cupboards. Make a note in your diary at a future time (in one month, six months, whatever feels appropriate to you) to check on the box. Try to remember what is in it before you open it. The chances are you will have forgotten, in which case it rather proves the point that you don't really need any of those things. Your life has gone on perfectly well without them. You could even do a deal with yourself – anything you can remember and still feel you have a genuine use for you can keep; anything else gets the shove! If this feels too extreme for you, then just open the box and seriously review the contents again, bearing in mind that you haven't needed any of them for the entire time they've been in storage.

One woman was so worried that she might regret getting rid of something that she bagged it all up in three large dustbin bags and slept with them in her bedroom for three nights. She figured that if there was anything in there that she would miss, she would have been out of bed in the middle of the night, rummaging through the bags to retrieve it. But she slept peacefully every night and on the fourth morning she happily dumped the lot and didn't miss a thing.

Tidying

If your clutter is more of the messy variety rather than things which need sorting and chucking, here's a very good way to get the momentum going to help you tidy your home and keep it that way.

Start in one corner of the room. Pick up any object at random that needs to be put away. Let's say it's a T-shirt. Start talking to yourself out loud in a kind of rhythmic chant, describing what you are doing. 'I am picking up the T-shirt and I'm walking to the wardrobe. I'm opening the door and I'm hanging it in on a hanger.' Then go and get some more items from the same corner. 'I'm picking up the newspaper and putting it in the bin. I'm picking up the book and I'm putting it on the shelf.' And so on.

All your sentences need to have a similar rhythm and be in two parts: da-da-dee-da-dee-da and da-da-dee-da-dee-da. It is this rhythm which carries you along and makes the task enjoyable and fun. Kids love tidying this way. It also means that your mental dialogue is already full, so you don't get stuck in your usual indecisiveness or bogged down in details. You just get into the rhythm and go with it. You start in one corner and just work your way across the space until it is clear.

GETTING CLUTTER OFF THE PREMISES

Don't do all that work and not take the final step of getting it off the premises. This is a crucial part of clutter clearing!

Rubbish and Recycling   Clutter you have decided is rubbish or can be professionally recycled is usually the easiest and quickest to dispose of. Hire a skip to take rubbish away, load the stuff into a car or van and drive it to the local rubbish tip or recycling centre yourself, or put it in your dustbin for the refuse or recycling service to collect. It feels very satisfying to get it out of your home as soon as you can.

Gifting   Gifts to friends, relations, charity shops, institutions and other deserving causes generally take longer to dispose of. You may have to wait until you see a particular friend or pass a particular charity shop, school, library, hospital, etc. If you choose this option, set yourself a date (say, the end of the month) by which you will have gifted whatever is your relevant **Recycling** box, or do a deal with yourself that you will consign it to the trash heap. Don't misunderstand me. I am wholeheartedly in favour of ex-clutter being given to people who will use and appreciate it, but my experience is that most junk designated as gifts just sits in boxes or bags and never makes it out of the door. Until you have become experienced at clutter clearing, it may not be wise to allow yourself the luxury of gifting. Just get rid of it as fast as possible.

Returning Things   This can also take a while. You have to contact the people they belong to and request, plead or insist that they take them out of your space. Set a date a reasonable time hence and if they haven't collected the stuff by then, let them know that you will dispose of it in any way you see fit. Alternatively, you may decide to mail or deliver the items back yourself.

Selling   This can take even longer. It's generally not a good bet for a first-time clutter clearer, unless you have a bulk purchaser, or decide to have a car boot or garage sale (an excellent idea).

Exchanging and Bartering   This is even more difficult unless you happen to know someone who is looking for exactly what you have and has exactly what you want, or you contact an organisation which specialises in exchanges or barters. Set yourself a deadline and if you haven't found the exchange or barter you want to make by that date, agree to sell it, give it away, trash it, or whatever.

Repairing, Altering, Renovating, etc.   These can take the longest time of all and are by far the dodgiest bet. The chances are very strong that they will still be unrepaired, unaltered and unrenovated this time next year or, in fact, this time next decade. Be particularly wary of keeping obscure items you have convinced yourself you will someday transform into something useful, and items you are keeping until you have something to go with them to make them useful. Dream on!

Treating Yourself

My whole intention in writing this book has been to make the benefits of clutter clearing so attractive that you will overcome the inertia of keeping it. Adopt the attitude that you will treat yourself to clearing out your clutter! Later, when you have experienced the benefits, you will want to treat yourself more often. As one woman said to me, 'I never realised one could get just as much pleasure from getting rid of material possessions as from acquiring them in the first place!'

Remember, you don't need to aim for perfection. Just aim to deal with the clutter that is clogging up your space and then get on with your life.

17

STAYING CLUTTER-FREE

One man e-mailed me to tell me, 'I am busy clearing the clutter. Now I see more clutter than ever. I laugh at myself. I look in a drawer for something and see the mess. I stop and clean out the drawer. I feel better after each project is done'.

Some weeks later he e-mailed me again: 'I came in from a skiing trip last night and had four bags of stuff. Before I left this morning it all had to be put away because it was driving me nuts seeing the clutter'.

This man has definitely integrated clutter clearing into his life! The knack to staying clutter-free is to change your hoarding habits.

A Place for Everything and Everything in its Place

I remember reading once about a very wealthy Arabian family who regularly travelled between four different cities in their country. The husband travelled to conduct his business, and his entire family accompanied him. Finding it very disorientating to be so much on the move, he used his wealth to build an identical mansion in each of the four locations, and had each home decorated and furnished exactly the same. Not only that, but when any member of the family went shopping for clothes they purchased four of each item, one of which was dispatched to each of the different homes, to be hung in exactly the same place in each of the four identical wardrobes. So, no matter where they were, whenever anyone went to open their wardrobe, it was the same.

As a frequent commuter between several destinations myself, I was fascinated by this description. An ordered home means an ordered mind. Whatever your personal situation, it is important to get organised so that the mundane level of your life supports you.

Getting Organised

One of the most amusing sights in the world is a myopic person hunting for their glasses! After you have cleared your clutter from table tops they will, of course, be much easier to spot, but make it really easy on yourself by allocating them a resting place all of their own. Do the same with your keys, wallet, slippers and any other items you find yourself repetitively searching for.

Here are some other tips to make your life simpler:

★ Store similar things together.
★ Keep things near where you are going to use them (for example, store your vases near to where you arrange flowers).
★ Put the things you use most often in the easiest to get to places.
★ Make it easy for things to be put where they belong and then they won't get disorganised or cluttered.
★ Label boxes so you know what is in them.
★ Arrange the clothes in your wardrobe according to colour (they look more appealing this way too).

Buy a Filing Cabinet and Use It

We live in the information age. Everyone needs a place for keeping paper records, whether relating to home or business, and the best way to deal with this is to purchase a filing cabinet. Some modern cabinets are very nice looking. You can store bits of paper which belong together in files and find them far more easily than if you keep them stacked in a pile. Create different categories. If you find yourself with a piece of paper you need to keep and you can't figure out which of your files to put it in, don't just leave it on the unsorted pile –

figure out a new category and create a new file for it. Files which become suspiciously fat either need breaking down into separate, smaller files or you need to do some weeding of outdated documents. Files which stay persistently thin are either redundant or need integrating into larger ones. At least once a year, go through your filing cabinet and throw out anything which is no longer relevant.

Storing Things

The purpose of storage space is somewhere to temporarily put things which are currently not in use. A good example of this is Christmas decorations, which are used only once a year. Winter clothes can be stored during summer months and vice versa. Then there are such things as camping equipment that is only used every other year. Just don't store too many things and leave them there indefinitely without ever using them. That's when the energy starts to stagnate.

Some things you are obliged by law to keep for a certain amount of time, such as tax records and supporting documents. Find out the statutory requirement in your country. If it is, say, seven years, then file your papers in separate tax years so that as the new tax year dawns, you can heave the records from eight years ago into the bin. Most people find this tremendously satisfying!

Stopping Clutter Before it Starts

You can save yourself a lot of clutter clearing by adopting these new habits:

★ Think twice before you buy. Decide before you purchase anything where you are going to keep it and what you are going to use it for. If your answers to either of these questions are vague then you are about to purchase clutter. Desist from buying.

★ Empty the rubbish bins in your home daily, either at the end of each day or first thing in the morning, whichever suits you best. And make sure you have enough of them around the place so that when you want to fling something you can!

★ Ban the use of the words 'for now' in your mind and in your speech. Whenever you say you are putting something somewhere 'for now', it means you are planning to go back to it again later and put it in its proper place. Get into the habit of putting it in its place straight away.

★ If you know you are prone to hoarding, make a new rule for yourself: 'When something new comes in, something old goes out'. At least your clutter will be changing, even if it's not decreasing yet!

Hire a Professional to Help You

In America they are called professional organisers. I call the people I train clutter clearing consultants (CCC's). I write my books to teach people how to help themselves, but maybe you have so much clutter that you really do need professional help to get you started and keep you at it. My website address and the telephone numbers of my offices are at the back of this book.

18

CLUTTER CLEARING YOUR BODY

A natural progression of clearing clutter in your home is clearing the clutter inside the temple of your own physical body. People who collect clutter on the outside tend to collect it on the inside too, but whereas clutter on the outside can hamper your progress in life, clutter on the inside can have even more serious health-threatening or even life-threatening consequences.

The human body is a highly sophisticated processing machine. It takes stuff in, assimilates from it what it needs and churns out the rest through five main eliminatory systems – the colon, kidneys, skin, lungs and lymphatics – and also several subsidiary systems such as the eyes, ears, navel, nails, hair and, in women, the vagina. All these channels are designed to efficiently remove the clutter of undesirable toxins from the body.

COLON CLEANSING

At the end of the 'Clearing clutter' chapter of my first book, I included a section entitled 'Clear out your colon'. In just two concise paragraphs I outlined the principles of herbal colon cleansing and recommended a UK supplier of the herbal formulae I have used myself for many years with great results. I didn't contact the supplier to let him know I would be including his details and was astonished to hear a year later that he had been deluged with enquiries ever since from readers of my book. I am therefore including here a much longer and more complete section on this and other related topics since there is obviously a good deal more interest in it than I first supposed!

Why You Need to Clear Your Colon

Most western people don't even know that they need to clear their colons. They believe that the way they feel and the level of health they tolerate is the way things are, but in actual fact they no longer know what 'normal' feels like. Years of eating unnaturally processed, cooked, frozen, canned, irradiated and preserved food have contributed to this. Undertakers report that corpses rarely need to be embalmed these days –

we unwittingly eat so many preservatives that our bodies now take much longer to decompose after death!

Curled up inside the human abdomen is about 22ft (6.5m) of small intestine, leading to 5ft (1.5m) of large intestine (also known as the colon or bowel). So that you can visualise it, the large intestine is about $2^1/_2$ in (5.5cm) in diameter ... or, rather, it is supposed to be.

The first picture (see over) shows a healthy colon; the second shows what happens to the colons of most people following a western diet, which is well documented as being the unhealthiest in the world. It is likely that many of you reading this book have colons which are distorted and coated in stagnant, impacted faeces. Just about everyone who eats western food does. Certainly, if you have a thick waistline or bulging abdomen, this is very likely to be the case.

Mucoid plaque forms in the colon, partly as a residue of eating mucus-forming foods and partly because our bodies naturally secrete mucus in our intestines as a defence mechanism against toxins. The mucus can be cleared away by pancreatic juices but mucus-forming food now forms such a huge percentage of the western diet that the pancreas cannot cope. Layers of plaque build up throughout the length of the intestinal tract, and then compact and harden. With our modern-day child-rearing practices, this all begins when you are an infant! NASA research scientists have discovered traces of mother's milk in adult colons, indicating that many people carry impacted faecal matter in their colons all their lives.

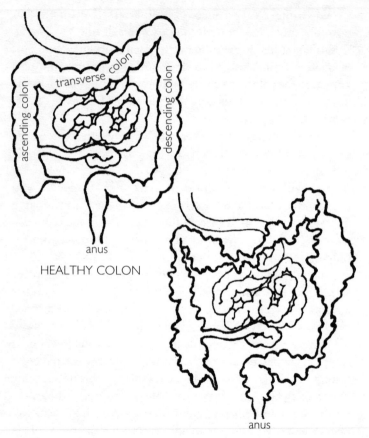

Healthy and unhealthy colons

A healthy colon contains residual friendly bacteria which weigh up to 5 lb (2.25 kg); encrusted colons have been found at autopsy to weight 40 lb (18 kg) or more. Sometimes there is so much putrid matter that parts of the colon expand from 2½ in (5.5 cm) in diameter to an obscene 10 or even 20 in (22 or 44 cm) in very obese people, leaving a channel of only about a pencil's width in the centre through which excreted matter can pass. The colon becomes permanently toxic and all manner of health problems result as these poisons seep into your bloodstream and find their way to all parts of your body.

If you consume, or have ever consumed, meat, poultry, fish, dairy products, sugar, processed food of any kind, chocolate, caffeine, soft drinks or alcohol, then you will certainly have mucoid plaque and benefit from colon cleansing. Even vegans usually need to do it because of mucus build-ups from soy and grain foodstuffs (soy beans are the most mucoid-forming of all plants). All traditional cultures, whether meat-eating or vegetarian, have certain herbs they take from time to time to cleanse their intestinal tracts.

In the same way that each part of your home is connected to an aspect of your life, so each section of your colon is connected to a part of your body (see Dr Richard Anderson's book, *Cleanse and Purify Thyself*). Hence many herbalists advocate colon cleansing as the cure for 90 per cent of all diseases and I certainly have found it to be enormously beneficial in terms of both preventative and curative healing. It works because you not only clean up your internal sewer system, but in the process of doing so, all manner of emotional issues which may have been buried in there for years come to the surface and get released. It is in the emotional resolution that the real healing takes place.

Eating and Excreting

Eating and excreting is the most natural process in the world, yet most western people are totally out of touch with their own bodies. In particular, they feel disgusted at the thought of their own excrement. I have noticed that Balinese babies get toilet trained much quicker than western babies, and I think this is to do with the fact that they are not trussed up in nappies so they get to figure out what is going on much quicker.

From all my research into this 'not-to-be-discussed-in-polite-company' topic over the years, I have concluded that one of the daftest things ever invented is the western sit-down toilet. The squatting position adopted by the millions of people who live in the east opens the colon and makes it much easier to evacuate the bowel than sitting doubled up on a western toilet. I think this, together with diet, is a major reason why colon diseases are so common in the west and so rare in the east. (Note: A useful health tip if you use a western toilet is to sit up straight and raise both arms high above your head – this opens up the intestinal tract in a similar way to squatting.)

Maybe this is all getting a bit much for you. I do appreciate how distasteful some people find these topics. However, I consider colon cleansing to be crucial to preventive medicine. If your colon is clear, your body thrives and your life works. If the colon is clogged, it will affect everything you do. If you need any more convincing, Dr Richard Anderson tells of a very revealing experiment:

> *Alexis Carrel of the Rockefeller Institute and recipient of the Nobel Prize <u>was able to keep tissue cells alive indefinitely</u> by nutritious feedings and by washing away tissue excretions. The cells grew and thrived as long as the evacuations were removed. Unsanitary conditions resulted in lower vitality, deterioration and death. He kept a chicken heart alive for 29 years until someone failed to cleanse its excretions!*

Constipation and Diarrhoea

The general rule is, 'new meal in, last one out'. So if you do not feel the urge to have a bowel movement within half an hour of finishing eating a meal, you are constipated. And long-term diarrhoea is just as much of a problem because it means your colon is so laden with harmful bacteria (and probably parasites too, which adore putrid, decaying matter) that it is constantly irritated.

The following symptoms are also indicative of colon problems: intestinal rumblings, stomach pains, smelly farts, feeling that even healthy food doesn't nourish you properly (poor nutrient absorption), bad breath, body odour and smelly feet. There will also be a sense of generally feeling below par.

If you are still in doubt, take the sunflower seed test. Put a handful of sunflower seeds in your mouth, chew them as little as possible, and then swallow them. Now wait until they appear at the other end! If your intestinal transit time is about ten hours, you are in good shape. If it is longer, you could use some colon cleansing to clear the encrustation. Some people find they have to wait three or four days before the sunflower seeds appear! One woman wrote to tell me how pleased she and her husband were to notice the sunflower seeds emerging only twelve hours later ... and then they noticed they appeared again and again and again over the next three days. So you need to keep watching!

The Ideal Bowel Movement

Now here is some information which it is difficult to find in any book. Here is what an ideal bowel movement will be like after you have done thorough colon cleansing:

★ Comes out easily, noiselessly and within seconds.
★ Emerges all in one piece and floats in the toilet pan (mucus makes it sink).
★ Is light brown in colour.
★ Doesn't pong much.
★ Is smooth, cylindrical and not compacted.
★ Breaks up easily when the toilet is flushed.

This is why I say that reading material kept near the toilet is a sure sign of constipation – if you have time to read anything while you're in there, you're in bad shape!

The Benefits of a Clean Colon

So far I have outlined the dire results of a filthy colon so now here are some of the positive benefits of having a clear-out. Most people find that after doing it once, they love the results so much that they make it a regular annual event. After colon cleansing you can expect to:

★ Feel and look healthier (better skin tone, fewer wrinkles, stronger nails, shinier hair, etc.);
★ Feel more buoyant and energetic;
★ Have a stronger immunity to disease;
★ Derive more nourishment from your food and have less desire to junk out;
★ Experience more love, joy and happiness in your life;
★ Be more flexible in your approach to life;
★ Be happy to let go of the old and welcome the new;
★ Enjoy more satisfying sex (because you do not have the internal pressure of an overburdened colon).

Louise Hay, in her book *Heal Your Body* gives the metaphysical cause of bowel problems as 'fear of letting go of the old and no longer needed' and recommends the affirmation, 'I freely and easily release the old and joyously welcome the new'. As a practical measure to reinforce this, allow yourself in future, when practically possible, to go to the toilet as soon as you feel the urge instead of making yourself wait as long as possible, as so many people do. In this way you re-educate yourself to physically let go easily and quickly, rather than holding on to things until you are forced to act, and this filters through to mental, emotional and all other aspects of your life.

Herbal Colon Cleansing

Herbal colon cleansing, done in conjunction with a regenerative nutrition programme (there is no point in clearing junk out at one end while shovelling the same kind of stuff back in again at the other!) produces remarkable results. Allow one month for every year of your life you have been eating sugar, mucus-forming or other junk food.

Never use laxatives. They irritate and weaken the bowel, Colonics are useful as an aid to cleansing the body during fasting but are no substitute for the deep cleansing and rebuilding properties of colon herbs.

It is always best to work with a qualified herbalist. The process invariably brings up emotional issues which you may need support with and you may also want reassurance when your body starts evacuating what looks like bits of old rubber tyres! As one man told me, 'It is horrifying to see what comes out but very satisfying to see it go.'

I have included a list of useful books to read on this subject in the Bibliography section at the back of the book, and in the Resources section there are details of suppliers of Dr Christopher's herbal formulae, which are the ones I have found to be most effective.

Be sure to get professional advice if you are pregnant, breast-feeding, elderly, chronically ill, weak or debilitated.

Parasite Removal

There is a modern myth that worms and other parasites are only found in third world countries. They also abound in the west, and colon cleansing is a vital part of clearing them from your body. Read Dr Hulda Clark's *The Cure for All Diseases* for detailed information about this. It may well be a revelation to you just how often parasites are implicated in poor health.

Fasting

After months of being 'on the road' teaching workshops in the west, eating in restaurants, sleeping in hotels and travelling on planes, it is pure bliss to get back home to Bali, and have the time and space to do some honest-to-goodness juice fasting. Nothing revitalises and energises me more than fasting on pure, organic, freshly-juiced fruit or vegetables and, best of all, pure water.

Here is how it works. When you eat food, it takes a lot of energy for your body to digest it. When you fast on juices all your internal organs get a holiday, so all that surplus energy is available for repair and revitalisation. I believe the dumbest thing a person can do when they are seriously ill is to eat anything at all. Animals know this. They never eat when they are sick.

Except in the case of medical emergencies, it is always best to do colon cleansing before juice fasting. Most of the unpleasant side-effects people report from fasting are simply due to autointoxication from putrid matter caught in their own colon when it stops moving. And for those of you who dread feeling hungry if you fast, here is a tried and tested tip: for the first day or two, mix generous quantities of spirulina powder with your juice or take spirulina in tablet form (several dozen during the day). It is the most complete protein known, is excellent for toning the bowel and you will not feel hungry in the slightest if you take it. By the end of Day Two, all hunger pangs will have ceased.

The ultimate in fasting is the pure water fast. Again, except in medical emergencies, it is usually best to work up to this rather than taking just water from Day One. Gradually dilute your juice more and more until you are taking only pure water.

It is vital that you seek the help of a qualified professional and read widely on this subject before attempting a fast. You need to know how long to fast, what to fast on and especially how to break a fast. Breaking one too quickly or with the wrong type of food can have serious, even fatal, consequences. However, done correctly, fasting is one of the most exhilarating experiences you can imagine. It is such a treat to give your internal organs a chance to rest and for you to experience what it is like not to stuff your emotions down with food all the time. You will discover new depths of passion and vitality in your life!

THE KIDNEYS

Our body weight is made up of approximately 70 per cent water and yet many people barely consume one or two glasses of pure water a day. All cells contain water, the blood is 90 per cent water, even our bones are 22 per cent water. Its presence is fundamental to life and good health, to transport oxygen and other nutrients to cells and to take toxins away from cells.

So my message is: drink water. It is the best thing you can drink. Water cleanses and purifies, bringing you greater clarity in your life. Ideally, drink $3\frac{1}{2}$ pints (2 litres) of water a day. Freshly juiced fruit and vegetables are also good, in addition to water. However, tea, coffee, sugared soft drinks and alcohol put a tremendous strain on the body, especially the kidneys, liver, pancreas and colon, and are to be avoided. They are largely composed of water but they also contain strong dehydrating agents!

You will know if you are drinking enough water by the very simple God-given mechanism called thirst. Do not ignore it. By the time you feel thirsty, your cells are already dehydrated. You can also check the colour of your urine. Dark yellow urine means you are giving your kidneys a hard time. Very pale yellow or almost colourless urine means you are well hydrated.

There is also an art to when to drink fluids. It is best to drink about half-an-hour before you eat and then wait for one-and-a-half to two hours after eating before you drink again. Otherwise you dilute the digestive juices in your stomach, which causes internal havoc (the food spoils and ferments, producing acidosis, which affects all body functions). When you chew your food properly you don't need water to wash it down with.

If you discover you enjoy colon cleansing, you may decide to do a herbal kidney cleanse once a year as well to keep these vital water-filtration organs in good shape.

THE LUNGS

Breathe deeply to allow your lungs to do their job of eliminating toxins through the lungs. Most westerners sub-ventilate, taking in just enough air to sustain themselves. This is all tied in with feelings of low self-esteem: 'I don't deserve', 'I'm not good enough', and so on. If you feel like this, your shoulders will slouch forward as your body unconsciously tries to protect your heart region, and this will restrict your breathing still further.

Straighten your spine. Take heart. It is your birthright to

live life to the full. With every breath you take, you are saying 'yes' to life, 'yes' to love, 'yes' to joy, happiness and abundance. Learn from the native people of the world or watch a newly arrived western baby and discover that correct breathing is not the shallow type into the upper chest but deep from the diaphragm, allowing the internal organs to get massaged with every breath. Breathe through your nose, never through your mouth. Greet each new day by taking very deep breaths, opening your arms wide and filling your lungs to maximum capacity, affirming life and clearing the clutter of stagnant residual air from the bottom of your lungs. Remember also to breathe when you eat, to oxygenate your food.

Other ways you can help your lungs are to take vigorous walking exercise, avoid mucus-forming food which clogs them (see page 153), avoid pollutants and, of course, stop smoking if you haven't already. Find a book which shows pictures of how grotty the lungs of smokers are if you want further incentive to quit – it's quite a shock!

THE LYMPHATIC SYSTEM

The lymphatic system cleanses all the tissues of the body. The blood has the heart to pump it around the body but the lymphatic system relies entirely on the action of the lungs and the muscles of the body, which is why regular exercise is so important. Walking, swimming, other forms of gentle exercise and trampolining are excellent ways to get the lymph moving. Most types of massage are also helpful. So is dry skin brushing (see the next section about the skin).

One very important consideration is to avoid tight clothing, which will obstruct the flow of lymph in the body. In their book *Dressed to Kill*, Sydney Ross Singer and Soma Grismaijer warn of the health effects which can result from lymph restriction and toxic build-ups caused by women wearing bras, not to mention 'tight pants syndrome' in men.

From a survey of over 4,700 American women between 1991 and 1993, they concluded that 'the average American woman is 19 times more likely to develop breast cancer than is a woman who wears a bra for less than twelve hours daily' and 'women who wear their bras all the time have a 113-fold increase in breast cancer when compared with women who wear their bras less than twelve hours daily'. They note that in countries of the world where women have only recently begun wearing bras, breast cancer is only now becoming known.

Underwired bras, especially the sexy push-up variety, inhibit lymph drainage even more and it is my belief that the metal also acts as a kind of antenna to conduct harmful electromagnetic fields from computers and other electrical appliances into the delicate breast tissue, contributing to the likelihood of breast cancer. Women working as computer operators, sewing machinists and in other jobs where their breasts are in close proximity to the electromagnetic fields of electrical equipment are most at risk, and definitely need to avoid wearing underwired bras.

THE SKIN

Skin is amazing. Each square inch consists of about 19 million cells, 600 sweat glands, 90 oil glands and 65 hairs, serviced by 19,000 nerve cells, 19ft (5.7m) of intricately woven blood vessels, and populated by tens of millions of microscopic bacteria.

Functioning at capacity, our skin is designed to eliminate one-third of the body's waste products but in reality most people's skin functions poorly. Synthetic toiletries clog the pores and synthetic fabrics (lycra, nylon, polyester and so on) severely inhibit this natural process, particularly undergarments, which are worn closest to the skin. It is far better to wear natural fabrics – pure cotton is the best, and linen, silk and wool are also good – and avoid washing them with harsh biological washing powders, the residues of which are absorbed through your pores.

To help the skin, take exercise, saunas or turkish baths to sweat out toxins and do daily dry skin brushing to remove dead skin cells, clear out lymph, stimulate the glands and prevent premature ageing. This is best done in the morning before bathing. Always brush towards the heart and use a natural bristle brush, which can be purchased in most health food shops. It feels fantastic!

19

CLEARING MENTAL CLUTTER

If you have physical clutter in your home, you will also have clutter in your mind. Here is what to do about some of the most common forms of mental clutter.

Stop Worrying

I once heard it said that worry is like a rocking horse – no matter how fast you go, you never move anywhere. Worry is a complete waste of time and creates so much clutter in your mind that you cannot think clearly about anything.

The way to learn to stop worrying is by first of all understanding that you energise whatever you focus your attention on. Therefore, the more you allow yourself to worry, the more likely things are to go wrong! Worrying becomes such an ingrained habit that you have to consciously train yourself differently. Whenever you catch yourself having a worry up (and ask those close to you to also help point out to you when you're at it again), stop and change your thoughts. Focus your mind more productively on what you *do* want to happen, rather than what you are worried might happen, and dwell on what's already wonderful in your life, so more wonderful stuff will come your way.

Make a list right now of all the things you worry about so that you'll spot them next time they turn up in your mind for a free rocking-horse session.

Stop Criticising and Judging

This is a total waste of effort, especially when you realise that everything you criticise and judge about others is something you don't like about yourself. The greatest critics are those who believe deep down, for whatever reason, that they themselves aren't good enough. Change these inner insecurities and the desire to demean others will magically melt away.

The other important thing to understand is that as humans we see only a segment of reality in the greater cosmic scheme of things so we are really never in a position to judge anyone or anything. A low-life street drunk may in essence be the kindest, sweetest soul you could ever meet, but if you judge him simply by appearances or get on some high moral platform about his behaviour, you will miss that quality completely.

Don't clutter your mind with these pointless poison arrows. Instead, silently send blessings to everyone you meet and be amazed how they in turn respond to you from the best of themselves.

Stop Gossiping

Constantly titillating yourself by gossiping about others clutters your psyche and only shows how little of consequence is happening in your own life. Live and let live. Refuse to indulge in or listen to gossip or scandal in any form, and make it a point of integrity that you never say anything about anyone that you would not say to their face.

Stop Moaning and Complaining

Moaning, complaining and blaming everything and everyone else for what is happening in your life clutters your speech and thoughts in such a way that most people don't even want to be around you. Focus on what you are grateful for and the gods will heap more goodies upon you. Keep moaning and groaning and you'll be on your own.

Stop Mental Chatter

Psychologists estimate that the average person has about

60,000 thoughts per day. Unfortunately, 95 per cent of those thoughts are exactly the same as the thoughts you had yesterday. And these are the same as the thoughts you had the day before yesterday. And so on. In short, most of your mental process is unproductive, repetitive chatter going nowhere.

Another problem is the constant babble of external stimuli that is so prevalent in the western lifestyle. So many people have the TV or radio constantly turned on 'for company', or spend their time reading trashy novels, aimlessly surfing the Net, and so on. Then suddenly one day you are old or sick and you realise you have done nothing with your life. All your thoughts are other people's thoughts and you have no idea who you really are or what the purpose of your life might be.

When is the last time you had a genuinely new, completely original thought? The sad fact is that many people just continue day after day in the same old groove, filling their minds with the mundane clutter of day-to-day existence.

Make it a priority to have clarity in your life and fine-tune that clarity daily. Make space for some form of meditative practice you enjoy or create definite time for quality 'moodling', a lovely term I have borrowed from Gill Edwards, author of *Living Magically*, to describe time spent gently wombling, with nowhere you have to be and nothing you have to do, which quietens the chatter and allows you to be open to higher wisdom and guidance, and greater creativity.

Tidy Up Loose Ends

Get into the habit of tying up loose ends as you go. As an example, supposing you are talking with a friend and they have a useful telephone number they want to give you. They have it with them, but they offer to phone you with it tomorrow. It's amazing how often people put off tomorrow what they can quite easily do today, and how much of an energy drain it is having loose ends to remember. Take the phone number then and there, and that is one less thing you have to do in your life!

Tidy up other loose ends such as repaying any money you owe, returning anything you have borrowed, running an errand you have said you will do, and anything else that is nagging away in the back of your mind to be done. Every unfulfilled promise or commitment has a call on your energy and pesters you to do it. If you know you can't keep your promise, it is far better to contact the person and let them know, rather than just let the situation drift.

Here's an interesting thing I have found from my own life experience, as a result of having dumped the word 'should' from my vocabulary. Supposing I have promised to meet a friend on Thursday evening to go and see a movie we both want to see. As Thursday approaches, I feel less and less inclined to go out that night. I can do one of two things: I can keep my promise and go because I said I would and therefore should, or I can call my friend and cancel or postpone the date. Ninety per cent of the times I cancel or postpone I have found that the other person was also wanting to do the same but didn't want to let me down, so it works perfectly for both of us. The other 10 per cent of times people get a bit upset or put out but if they are honest with themselves, it is not usually me that has upset them. The problem is generally their own inflexibility or that I have triggered the memory of a much deeper upset from the past. See the next chapter for an understanding of upsets.

Clear Your Communications

Whom do you have unresolved issues with? Think for a moment. Imagine yourself in a social setting. Can you think of anyone in your life who, if they were to walk in the door, would immediately produce a feeling of uncomfortability in your body? Who would make you feel that the room wasn't big enough for the two of you, because there are tensions between you? You may not consciously remember these people, in fact you may actively try to keep them out of your thoughts, but your good old subconscious mind keeps track of them. Having unresolved communications in your life depletes your energy levels immensely.

If you sleep with someone, make especially certain that you keep your communications clear and resolved; otherwise you will be fighting psychic battles with each other all night and will wake up feeling like you need a good night's sleep.

Catch Up on Correspondence

Do you have letters which you keep meaning to write but never get round to? Every time you think about it and don't do it, your vitality levels drop. The longer you put it off, the more difficult it becomes to write the letter. If you just sit down and take the time to catch up on your correspondence, you will release huge amounts of energy for other purposes. Better still, switch to e-mail, which is so much faster and immediate, and therefore so much easier to stay current with.

Clear Your Diary

Do you find yourself with never enough time to do everything you want to do? Figure out the things you really enjoy doing and schedule them in your diary before anything else. Don't allow your mental taskmaster to dominate your life. These pleasures are what your spirit thrives on and if you just work, work, work without ever having time for yourself, or spend all your time looking after other people with no time to nourish yourself, pretty soon your spirit starts to wither and die. The first signs of this are general fatigue and diminishing health.

So put 'you' in your diary as a first priority and then fit everything around that. Years ago I started taking one day a week for myself out of my busy work schedule, and now I do it for up to six months a year. My time in Bali goes in my diary first and I slot everything else in around that.

Decluttering Your Mind for Restful Sleep

If you lead a busy life and have lots of 'things to do', you may find it difficult to switch off and relax. In particular, you may find your mind still active when you want to go to sleep. Here's a good tip. Keep a notebook and pen by your bed and just before you go to sleep, scribble down all the things you have to remember to do. Then just forget about them and go to sleep. If you wake up in the night with more things on your mind, just open one eye, scribble them down, and carry on sleeping. At first you may need to keep a small torch by your bed; with practise you can learn to write in the dark with your eyes shut.

The busier you are the more important it is to completely relax and take time off to rest and regenerate during the hours of the night. Once you have mastered this, you can then use your sleep time even more creatively. Instead of churning through problems and anxieties, use your sleep time to connect with your Higher Self and receive guidance (read Sanaya Roman's *Spiritual Growth: Being Your Higher Self*). You can hear the subtle messages from these higher realms if your mind and emotions are not constantly occupied with problems, and then you will have a lovely, peaceful night's sleep *and* wake up with answers!

Keep Yourself Up To Date

When everything is up to date in your life, you live in present time and can experience a real feeling of surfing with the energy of life. Do whatever it takes to catch up with yourself and then keep it that way. You will have more energy than you ever believed possible. Children are like this. They live in the moment, and we all know how much vitality they have!

20

CLEARING EMOTIONAL CLUTTER

Most people carry some form of emotional baggage. It prematurely ages us (I looked ten years younger after doing an intense year of personal work to clear out some of mine) and gets in the way of everything we want to do.

Upsets

If ever you are feeling really upset about something, that is one of the best times to go and clear some clutter. Don't bother to pull yourself together before you begin. Just go to the cupboard with tears streaming down your face, bawling your head off if necessary, and pull everything out and begin sorting it. You will be amazed how easy it is to sort clutter when you are in this condition. It almost seems to sort itself. You look at things you have been hoarding for years, and they seem so unimportant and obviously obsolete, and there is no emotional tug at all as you sling them in the bin. You will also be amazed how sorting the clutter helps to calm you and see what was upsetting you in a new perspective too. The act of letting go of the clutter also allows you to let go of your stuck feelings.

Realise that every upset is a set-up. What this means is that everything our lower emotion gets upset about is a situation that our Higher Self has set up to get our attention because something needs to change.

One teacher I studied with for a while used to say, if ever anyone was upset, 'Will it matter ten years from now?' You get to see the issue from the viewpoint of your future self looking back with hindsight, and the answer is nearly always 'no'.

You could say the same about most clutter. 'Will I have found a use for this within the next ten years?' For most things you have been holding on to for a long time, the answer is nearly always 'no'.

Grievances

One of the worst forms of emotional clutter is the type that results from grievances. Look deep within yourself to see who or what you need to forgive. Carolyn Myss, author of *Anatomy of the Spirit* and *Why People Don't Heal And How*

They Can, says that the root of illness lies in not letting go of feeling you've been treated unfairly by a person or a situation. You will know if this is the case because you will habitually remember this injustice many times a day, and it will have become so commonplace that you never even notice it any more. Decide now to forgive and let go.

Sometimes it happens that people become so entrenched in their grievances that they refuse even to talk to each other. I have come across instances in families and married couples where these prolonged silences continue for days, weeks, months, years and even for decades. Some people actually go to their graves with these feelings stuck in their bodies, and it's a pretty sure bet that's what finishes them off.

Sometimes these stuck feelings escalate to the level of disputes between whole families, groups or nations, which create cancers in the emotional fabric of society. Attempts to resolve the situation by physical violence continue until one of the protagonists is brought to their knees, or a third and greater power intervenes (called 'diplomatic intervention') to bring them both to their senses. Diplomacy can be defined as the art of harmonising stuck emotional energy.

If you are the silent sulky type, understand that this may hurt the other person as you intend it to do, but it hurts you even more. Take a course in human relationships and learn a better way to handle your problems. Forgive and forget. Let go of your grievances and get on with your life.

Clear Out Your Flaky Friends!

Do you know people whom it always feels like an effort to talk to or who drain you when you are with them? Do you groan when you know so-and-so is calling to talk to you on the phone? I'm not talking here about good friends who are temporarily going through a rough patch or having a bad week! I am talking about negative people who are seriously past their 'sell-by date', whom you would like to be rid of but haven't had the guts to, or haven't got round to doing anything about it.

One fascinating thing I have discovered is that just about everyone has a few of these unwanted 'friends'. I spent an entire dinner party recently listening to the story of 'the houseguest from hell' who turned up uninvited year after year and foisted herself on these people. For some inexplicable reason, they never felt able to tell her how unwelcome she was, so every year they endured her awful cooking and overbearing behaviour, then complained about her ever-after to everyone they knew.

Take a minute now just to make a little list of people you know who really you'd rather not know any more. I'll pause the book while you do this.

Now here's the interesting thing: If you have a little list like this, and everyone has a little list like this, then – WHOSE LIST ARE <u>YOU</u> ON? Now there's some food for thought! Wouldn't it be best if we just got honest with one another about this and stopped these silly games?

There are billions upon billions of people in the world and you are free to select whom you choose to mix with. Choose kindred spirits who uplift and inspire you. The wonderful thing about having the courage to clear our all your mouldy old friends is that it creates the space for you to attract wonderful, vital new relationships, providing you have made new decisions about what you will and will not have in your life. Eventually you will find that flaky people, energy vampires and seriously negative individuals will not be in your life because your energy field feels too incompatible with their own – they know that their chances of getting a free energy feed-up at your expense are nil, so they don't even bother trying.

Moving on from Relationships

Sometimes you realise it is not just an acquaintance who has become clutter in your life, but the person you thought was your significant other. This happens because your lives have diverged and moved on to different paths, or you never were compatible in the first place. The truth is that you have become clutter in each other's lives, although sometimes only one of you can see that at the time.

You now have two choices: do nothing and wait for the relationship to crumble or explode apart on its own, or have the courage to act, to either reinvent or leave the situation. If you still love, respect and are good for each other, the chances are high that you can find a way for the relationship to continue, even though the form is sure to change in some way. Give it every chance of success, and if it is time for you to move on, you will know in your heart of hearts that this is so.

In many instances it is, indeed, time to move on, and you do yourself and your partner a great disservice if you prolong the agony by delaying doing this too long. Scary as it may seem, if it is the right thing for you to do, you will discover that right alongside your quivering fear is another quivering energy called excitement. This is your spirit thrilling at the prospect of the new opportunities which are about to open up in your life.

To help you in this transition, read Susan Jeffer's excellent books, *Feel the Fear and Do it Anyway* and *End the Struggle and Dance with Life*. And follow your gut feeling.

Letting Go of Emotional Armour

If your home is very cluttered you may also feel the need to wear serious quantities of jewellery, probably to the extent that you may feel only half-dressed if you go out without it. Like house clutter, jewellery worn in this way is a form of emotional armour. After clearing your home, you are likely to feel naturally inclined to reduce the amount you wear because you feel more confident and able to let the natural 'you' shine through.

21

CLEARING SPIRITUAL CLUTTER

Actually the whole of this book has been about this. It is about the process of clearing away all the clutter which obscures our vision, confuses or misleads us, and hinders us on our path. Each of us has a life purpose and it is my belief that we incarnate with the conscious awareness of that purpose and the intention of fulfilling it. Once incarnate, it then becomes increasingly more difficult to maintain this level of consciousness and slowly the knowledge slips away from us. Clearing clutter in all forms allows our original purpose in coming here to resurface and shine through. This brings with it immense clarity and a profound sense of knowing what to do.

The higher purpose of clearing clutter is therefore to clear the debris that prevents us from connecting with our Higher Self and with God.

This Special Time

We are fortunate to be alive in what the majority of spiritual teachers today believe is the most important time in human evolution in the history of our planet. It used to be that all the great knowledge of the world was held by just a few. Do you realise that nowadays you can attend a weekend workshop and learn the basics of what in centuries gone by would have taken years of dedicated apprenticeship to a master?

Holding on to things which keep us rooted in the past can therefore be totally counterproductive. When you think about how many times you are likely to have reincarnated to be here today, surely your eternal spirit is keen to be in present time, ready and able to go with what is happening now.

Calling You Back to You

In Bali, they have a special ceremony known as 'The Calling'. It is understood that as a person goes through life, parts of themselves may unfortunately fracture and split off. If this happens too much or, in the case of a sudden, traumatic event, too quickly, this can weaken the spirit of the person to a life-threatening extent. After being injured in a road accident, as an example, a vital part of the healing process is for the person to return with a priest to the place where it happened, to ceremonially purify the spot and call the part of their spirit they left there back to themselves.

A similar calling-back process happens when you clear the clutter in your life. As you release the things you no longer love or use, you call back to yourself the parts of your spirit which have been attached to them, and attached to the emotional needs and memories associated with those objects. In so doing, you bring yourself powerfully into present time. Your energy, instead of being dispersed in a thousand different, unproductive directions, becomes more centred and focused. You feel more spiritually complete and more at peace with yourself. All this comes from simply clearing clutter. Amazing, isn't it!?!

Let Go and Let God

To conclude this book, here is a marvellous affirmation I want to share with you, which I have used in my own life to great effect. It is:

All my needs are taken care of as I follow my Higher Path.

When you totally trust that all your needs are taken care of, they totally will be. Ingrain this affirmation into every cell of your being and you will never need clutter again.

Appendix

THE 21 STEPS TO BASIC SPACE CLEARING

Important Notes

★ *There is a great deal more to understand about each of these steps than there is room to explain in this book, but this will at least give you an idea of what is meant by my references to Space Clearing.*

★ *These techniques are designed only for personal usage. The training to learn to do Space Clearing on a professional basis is as involved and demanding as for other branches of Feng Shui, and goes far beyond what is given here.*

PREPARATION

1. Do not attempt Space Clearing if you feel any fear or apprehension. These techniques are perfectly safe but are designed for personal everyday use, not for the purposes of exorcism – leave that to trained professionals.

2. Obtain permission before doing Space Clearing in someone else's personal space.

3. Do Space Clearing when you feel physically fit and healthy, emotionally centred and mentally focused.

4. It is best not to do Space Clearing if you are pregnant, menstruating, or have an open flesh wound.

5. Take the time to think about what you want to have happen in your life. If you share the space with others it is best to consult them too.

6. For best results, physically clean and tidy the space, sweep, mop or vacuum it, and clear out clutter first.

7. Take a full bath or shower, or at least wash your face and hands.

8. Put food and drink away in cupboards or sealed containers.

9. Remove jewellery and other metallic objects from your person. Work barefoot if possible.

10. Work alone unless other people present fully understand what you are doing.

11. Work in silence without background music. Turn off

any fans and other non-essential loud or droning machinery.

12. Open a door or a window.
13. Locate an appropriate energy point and set up your Space Clearing equipment.
14. Roll up your sleeves and sensitise your hands.

BASIC SPACE CLEARING PROCEDURES

15. Take time to attune to the space. Mentally announce yourself and radiate your intention.
16. Starting at the main entrance, go around the inside perimeter of the space, sensing the energy. Use your hands and all your other senses too.
17. Light candles, burn incense, sprinkle holy water, and offer flowers and prayers to the guardian spirit of the house and the spirits of earth, air, fire and water. Call in the angels and your own personal guides and helpers (whatever feels appropriate to you).
18. Clap in corners to disperse static energy. Then wash your hands in running water (very important to remember to do this).
19. Purify the space with bells.
20. Shield the space.
21. Fill the space with intention, light and love.

Adapted from Karen Kingston's book: *Creating Sacred Space with Feng Shui.*

KAREN KINGSTON

For more information about any of the following, visit Karen's website or contact one of her offices listed on the next page:

Consultations   Karen conducts Clutter Clearing, Space Clearing and Feng Shui consultations around the world, and also has a directory of consultants whom she has personally trained to a very high standard.

Courses and Professional Trainings   Clutter Clearing, Space Clearing and Feng Shui courses, and professional Space Clearing and Clutter Clearing trainings take place in England, America, Bali and other countries.

Products   Request a copy of Karen Kingston's Space Clearing products brochure, featuring Balinese Space Clearing bells, harmony balls, and many other high quality items available only at her courses or by mail order.

Audio Tapes   Bring the material in Karen's books vividly to life with audio recordings from her most popular courses. Available by mail order from her offices.

UK Office   *(for enquiries from the UK and the rest of the world, except the USA and Canada)*
Karen Kingston Promotions
Suite 401, Langham House, 29 Margaret Street
London W1N 7LB, England
Tel in the UK: 07000 CLUTTER (i.e. 07000 258883) or 07000 SPACE CLEARING (ie. 07000 772232)
Tel/Fax from outside the UK: +44 7000 258883 or +44 7000 772232
e-mail: UKoffice@spaceclearing.com

Enclose a large, self-addressed, stamped envelope if you would like to receive information by snail mail and, if enquiring from overseas, enclose an international postal coupon which can be exchanged for postage stamps in the UK.

US Office   *(for enquiries from the USA and Canada)*
InnerSpace
1623 Stanford Street, Santa Monica, CA 90404, USA
Tel: +1 (310) 264 1843
Fax: +1 (310) 264 1846
e-mail: USoffice@spaceclearing.com

Website   www.spaceclearing.com
(a lively site, regularly updated, with profiles of consultants, details of Karen's courses and products, and the popular 'Ask Karen Kingston' page for readers' questions).

BIBLIOGRAPHY AND RECOMMENDED FURTHER READING

Other Books by Karen Kingston

Creating Sacred Space with Feng Shui (Piatkus, Great Britain, 1996 & Broadway Books, New York, 1997)

Feng Shui
Collins, Terah Kathryn, *The Western Guide to Feng Shui* (Hay House, 1996)
Spear, William, *Feng Shui Made Easy* (Thorsons, 1995)

Space Clearing
Linn, Denise, *Sacred Space* (Rider, 1995)

Clutter Clearing

Treacy, Declan, *Clear Your Desk!* (Century Business, 1992)

Healing and Metaphysics

Diamond, John, MD, *Life Energy and the Emotions* (Eden Grove Editions, Great Britain, 1997, an abridged version of *Life Energy*, Dodd Mead, New York, 1985)

Hay, Louise L., *Heal Your Body* (Hay House, 1988)

Hay, Louise L., *You Can Heal Your Body* (Hay House, 1987 and Eden Grove Editions, England, 1988)

Jeffers, Susan, *End the Struggle and Dance With Life* (Hodder, 1996)

Jeffers, Susan, *Feel the Fear and Do it Anyway* (Random House, 1997)

Myss, Caroline, PhD, *Anatomy of Spirit* (Bantam, 1996)

Myss, Caroline, PhD, *Why People Don't Heal And How They Can* (Harmony Books, New York, 1997)

Roman, Sanaya, *Spiritual Growth: Being Your Higher Self* (H. J. Kramer, 1989)

Sams, Jamie & Carson, David, *Medicine Cards* (Bear & Co Publishing, 1989)

Wilde, Stuart, *Infinite Self: 33 Steps to Reclaiming Your Inner Power* (Hay House, 1996)

Colon Cleansing and Better Health

Aïvanhov, Omraam Mikhaël, *The Yoga of Nutrition* (Prosveta S.A., 1982)

Anderson, Dr Richard, ND, NMD, *Cleanse and Purify*

Thyself (self published, 1988 – available from Healthforce Regeneration Systems, 16921-C Via de Santa Fe, Box 5005, Rancho Santa Fe, CA 92067-5005, USA. Tel: +1 619 756 5292. Fax: +1 619 756 9560.)

Clark, Hulda Regehr, PhD, ND, *The Cure for All Diseases* (New Century Press, CA, 1995)

Dufty, William, *Sugar Blues* (Warner Books, 1975)

Jensen, Bernard, DC, *Tissue Cleansing Through Bowel Management* (Bernard Jensen, California, 1981)

Gray, Robert, *The Colon Health Handbook* (Emerald Publishing, Nevada, 1980)

Sharan, Dr Farida, *Herbs of Grace* (Wisdom Press, 1994)

Singer, Sydney Ross & Soma Grismaijer, *Dressed to Kill: The Link Between Breast Cancer and Bras* (Avery Publishing Group, New York, 1995)

Obsessive–Compulsive Disorders

Dumont, Raeann, *The Sky is Falling: Understanding and Coping with Phobias, Panic, and Obsessive–Compulsive Disorders* – Chapter 12 (Norton, 1997)

Quotations

The Uncommon Wisdom of Oprah Winfrey: A Portrait in Her Own Words, edited by Bill Adler (Aurum Press, 1997)

Resources

Suppliers of Dr Christopher Herbal Colon
Formulae

Simmonds Herbal Supplies

UK enquiries   Freepost BR1396, Hove BN3 6FN   Tel:
Freephone 0800 298 6698   Fax: 01273 705120
International enquiries   12 Hove Business Centre, Hove BN3
6HA, England Tel: +44 1273 381937 Fax: +44 1273 705120
e-mail: sales@herbalsupplies.com
Internet: www.herbalsupplies.com

Healthforce Regeneration Systems

US Sales only   16921-C via de Santa Fe, Box 5005, Rancho
Sante Fe, California 92067-5005, USA
Order Line   Tel: (800) 357 2717
Customer Service/Information Line   Tel: +1 (619) 756 5292
Internet: www.healthforce.net
Note: Their products are similar to the Dr Christopher
formulae with a few extras in there too. US regulations
prohibit them from exporting colon herbs outside America.

SEND YOUR CLUTTER
CLEARING STORIES!

For many an entrenched hoarder, it is hearing the success stories of ex-clutterholics that motivates them to dig in and clear out. Write to Karen Kingston with your clutter clearing success stories at the following address. Include your written permission for Karen to publish your tale if you are happy to share it with the world.

Karen Kingston
Suite 401, Langham House
29 Margaret Street, London W1N 7LB
England
e-mail: clutter@spaceclearing.com

Visit Karen's website at **www.spaceclearing.com** to view a selection of the most inspiring stories she receives.

INDEX

Creating Sacred Space with Feng Shui
Karen Kingston
with a foreword by Denise Linn

Karen's bestselling book *Creating Sacred Space with Feng Shui* tells you how to use simple, effective techniques to clear 'stuck' energy and create sacred space in your home or workplace. Learn:

★ The 21 steps of basic space clearing
★ How to choose and consecrate a home
★ The immense benefits of a clutter-free life
★ How to safeguard yourself against geopathic and electromagnetic stress
★ Feng Shui placement of furniture, mirrors and crystals to enhance the flow of energy

and much more.

Creating Sacred Space with Feng Shui is published by Piatkus books, priced at £9.99. It is available at all good bookshops. To order direct, call free on 0800 454 819 or write to: Piatkus Books, FREEPOST 7 (WD 4505), London W1E 4EZ. Please do not include cash with your order. We accept cheques, postal orders, Visa/Mastercard, or American Express.